YOUTUBE MARKETING MANUAL

Video Marketing for

Businesses, Speakers,

Consultants, and More

Updated for 2014

MARC BULLARD

Copyright © 2014
Marc Bullard
YouTube Marketing Manual

ATTENTION: Don't want to read this highly informative book but still want all of the great tips and techniques?

No problem, get the same thing in video form here:
YouTube Marketing Mastery
https://www.udemy.com/youtube-marketing-mastery/

Thanks to my book reading Mom, chip eating Dad, husband supporting wife, and 2 awesomely crazy sons.

http://www.MarcBullard.com

http://www.MarcBullard.com

YouTube Marketing Manual

Welcome to the YouTube Marketing Manual. If you're thinking about starting a video marketing campaign or if you already have one that could use some work, this book is for you.

The YouTube Marketing Manual provides you step-by-step instruction on how to use virtually every feature of YouTube, and more importantly, on how to use it for marketing. No matter how proficient you are with YouTube's many features (or not) I'm sure there is something in this book you never knew. A few of the lessons provided in this book include:

• How important video marketing is now and **will** be in the future
• How to get better search engine positioning with videos
• How to upload and optimize your YouTube videos
• How to optimize and maximize your YouTube channel
• How to search for popular videos and what to do with them
• How to research trending videos
• How to find the next upcoming viral videos
• How to structure your videos
• What equipment you should use (it's cheaper than you think)
• Discover the most popular videos and what to do with them.
• Popular methods to help you discover new demographics
• Helpful tools to enjoy and customize YouTube videos
• Step-by-step instruction
• How to keep viewers coming back
• Much, much, more

Let's not be formal here. This book is written as if I'm training you myself. The sentences will be written as if I'm having a conversation with you. Hey, that's just my style. What can I say? How about, let's get started.

The Importance of Video

Video marketing is one of the fastest growing and most powerful ways to spread information around the Internet. Online video has become easier to use over the years with better quality players and more vivid video formats.

With the ever growing advancements in software and technology, you can get a consumer level camera and inexpensive video editing software to create informative productions to use on websites, advertising and marketing of your business.

If you think about using video as advertising, this is the cheapest and easiest time in all of history that anybody - a small business person, a person who doesn't even have a business yet, a kid with a skateboard on a trampoline or a multimillion dollar Internet Marketer – can all use the same tool, the Internet. You, Joe Blow, and Joe Millionaire - it's almost an even-leveled playing field. Not taking advantage of it is pretty crazy.

The Internet is not television. Remember that. If you think about television 20 years ago, that was really the only place to get commercials seen other than print ads. It was the only place that you could get motion, moving pictures, and your product or services seen. You had to pay a good chunk of change too. You still do.

You have to pay a ton of money to get your little 30-second promotional video, commercial, or whatever you want, on television. Compared to the cost of Internet hosting, paying for TV ad space is not a good idea. Look at the numbers of people who are watching a certain channel on TV compared to the number of people watching videos online.

http://www.MarcBullard.com

The numbers of people watching a TV channel at that time and seeing your commercial are not great. They are so small compared to how many views and how many people could watch your video on the Internet. Not to mention, when you are home watching TV, what do you usually do when a commercial comes on? You either mute the TV or get up and go get a snack, go to the bathroom, etc.

Online viewers are specifically looking for information on whatever your video has to offer. They aren't going to get up in the middle of your video. If they really had to, they'd pause it and come back. You are getting a focused group of viewers looking for your information instead of interrupting a TV show to throw who knows what type of ad in their faces.

People are now turning to YouTube to search for information more than they are typing in to Google to read about certain topics. How would you like to have your own station where you can show whatever you choose? You can, and you can have it for free. It's called your YouTube channel. If you have a YouTube account - and you should, it's free - you automatically have a YouTube channel. This channel is where only your videos are seen. There are no related videos from other people, there are no ads, there are just your videos and your information. You can even customize it to look exactly the way you want.

Wouldn't it be nice to have viewers going to your channel to watch what you have up there? They would be less inclined to click out to other sites and more inclined to watch more of your stuff. And the more videos of yours they watch, the greater chance they will buy something from you.

Videos Generate Traffic

Get high search engine positioning
One reason why videos generate traffic is they get high search engine positioning. And that is because the search engines are specifically looking for multimedia; it's called a Universal Search. They want to find all the different media that they can to give the searcher the best experience. In addition, they are especially looking for video. If you haven't made any videos yet, think about how many search engine robots have just passed you by because you didn't have a video to offer.

There could be 200 websites on the keywords 'horseback riding', and there could be five videos on horseback riding. Which do you think is going to have a greater chance of showing up on the first page of Google if someone is searching for horseback riding?

Remember, Google likes to give video suggestions. You'd have a much greater chance if you made a video on horseback riding. Out of those five, you have one of those competing videos, compared to 200 text based sites. Whatever you're niche is, make a video because there is a very good chance that there are many more written articles than videos on the same subject.

Get message out more dynamically
Another reason videos generate traffic is because people get excited. Videos are just more dynamic. Imagine a sales letter that says, "Sensational Sales, 50% off! Click here!" In video, you are talking. You're showing your products, you're selling yourself, and people go, "Hell yeah, I want to click on that!" And they do. You get your messages out more dynamically in the sense that you are using images, you're using audio, you can put text on there. So you have these three tools at your service to get the message out compared to just text.

http://www.MarcBullard.com

Embed code allows sharing

Video sharing sites make it very easy to pass your video around. The way they do this is with an embed code. The embed code can go on virtually any other website and your video can be viewed there. Sharing is one of the most powerful ways to get your video seen and spread. Embed codes help with the ease of sharing your video and also with increasing your views. Any time your video is embedded on a site other than Youtube and somebody watches it, Youtube counts that as a view. The more views you have, the better it looks in Youtube's eyes.

Clickable links in descriptions

Putting clickable links in the description box of video sharing sites gives your viewers the opportunity to go directly to the site you want them to go to. Sites like Youtube have specific places where clickable links are allowed. Make sure you put a link to your site in these areas. If you don't, then how are people going to buy your product?

How Can Videos Help You?

Provide testimonials

Everybody knows that testimonials are gold when it comes to selling your product. Well, video testimonials are platinum. Video testimonials work better because we can see the customer. We can see their face, we can see how excited they are for the product. We can see how thankful they are for the product.

Video testimonials add credibility because they are harder to fake. Anybody can write a great sounding testimonial, add a name of the 'customer', and put it up on their site. With a video testimonial, the person on screen helps other viewers relate. And once you can relate with a potential customer, it's a whole lot easier to sell to them.

http://www.MarcBullard.com

Show your product in action

A picture is worth 1000 words. Each second of video contains 30 still frames - or pictures - in it. You do the math. Using video to show your product in action is one of the smartest things you can do. Video lets you 'show' instead of 'tell'. Actually, video will let you 'show' AND 'tell' compared to just 'telling' with text.

Do you have a new program you designed and want to show people how easy it is to use? Use video. Have a book that is really exciting? Use video to create a book trailer. Do you offer consulting to large or small businesses? Use video to show what your services are. The options are limitless.

Use as sales promotion

Do you have a great deal that everybody needs to know about? Create a video that talks about this. Do you have a sales letter explaining everything possible about your product, and do you have to scroll forever to get to the bottom of it? Use a video and save yourself a lot of space.

Show your company profile

A great way to stay in the public eye even when you don't have any new products to sell is to use video to show your company profile. Your company could consist of just you or a myriad of employees. Either way, creating a short video saying what you are up to, what's coming up in the future, or even how well you did in the past, is another fantastic use of video.

Introduce your staff

If you have customers who will be dealing with staff members of yours, it can be a weird situation to only know them by email or by a voice on the phone. Showing your employees in a video gives your customers a face to match to the voice they've been dealing with. It makes your business have a personality. This can help customers feel 'connected' to your business, which in turn eases their minds when it comes time to purchase your next great product.

Bring in Ad Revenue

There are professional 'YouTuber's' out there that simply create content and get paid to have ads on their videos. You can do the same thing with your videos. The nice thing about ad revenue is that it can be extra income on top of the money you are making from selling your products/services.

Are you ready to get into video marketing? Well, let's start at the site that started it all...

YouTube

YouTube is the world's largest video sharing site; it's owned by Google, and it has surpassed Yahoo! as the second largest search engine. You read that right, a video sharing site is now the second largest search engine behind Google; and Google loves that fact. Why? Because Google owns YouTube and they both work hand in hand.

YouTube is more than just a site for sharing videos. It's trying very hard to be a full-fledged social networking site as well. With features such as adding friends, subscribers, comments, bulletins, viewer rating, and more, it isn't far off from becoming a giant marketing tool. Most people know what YouTube is but most don't know about all of the features given to each user.
Getting people to see your video is one of the most critical aspects of video marketing. The larger the number of viewers, the greater the chance they'll buy your product or go to your site.

Using videos is a great way to 'funnel' traffic, weeding out the people who were never going to purchase in the first place. YouTube gives you every opportunity to get your video seen, but most people don't know how to properly use the site's features.

http://www.MarcBullard.com

We're going to focus on two aspects of YouTube: using YouTube's features and then how to use these features for marketing. This book is going to look at how to use YouTube and what to do with this powerful marketing tool.

Interface

YouTube Home Page
Once you have logged in to YouTube, you will be taken to your home page. The home page contains many different modules that provide information.

YouTube's homepage is laid out in order make it easy to find all of your subscribed channel's videos. (More on subscribers later.) It also helps integrate social sites with your activity on YouTube as well as making suggestions to videos you may like.

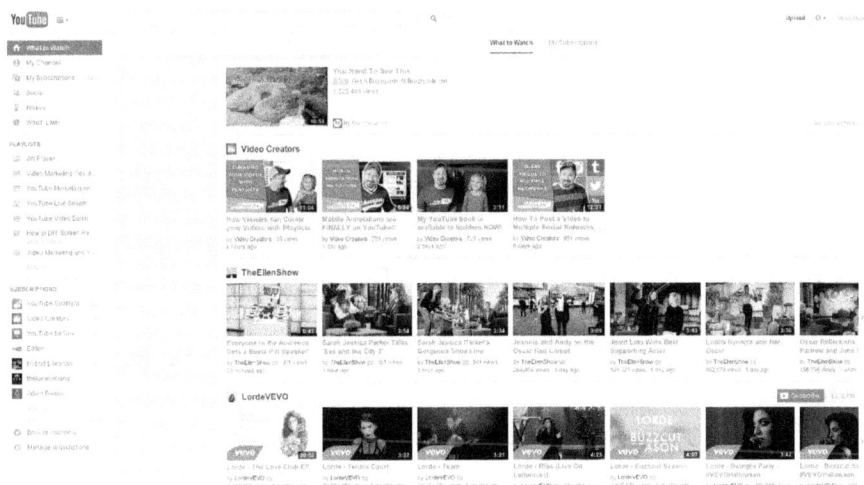

The home page is broken into 2 main columns: a Guide on the left and your Feed in the middle. The feed consists of two tabs: 'What to Watch' and 'My Subscriptions'. 'What to Watch' lists videos and channels you may be interested in watching.

http://www.MarcBullard.com

Starting in the upper left, you will see the YouTube logo and a button to show/hide the Guide. Below that you will have options for 'What to Watch', 'My Channel', 'My Subscriptions' and more.

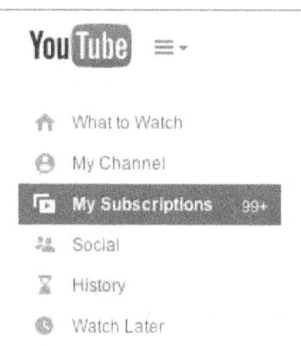

Clicking the YouTube icon in the upper left will show you the 'What to Watch' page by default. Below the YouTube icon is the 'What to Watch' link. This will take you to the same exact page.

Clicking 'My Channel' will take you to your very own YouTube channel. Your channel is very important and is discussed later in this book.

Next you see 'My Subscriptions'. Clicking this will bring you to a list of the YouTube channels you are subscribed to. This 'My Subscriptions' link takes you to the exact same place is if you were to click the 'My Subscriptions' tab in the upper middle of your feed. 'My Subscriptions' is also layed out in three modules: Guide in the left, Feed in the middle, and Recommended Channels on the right. If you are not subscribed to any channels, there won't be any information in this feed.

Below 'My Subscriptions' is 'Social. Clicking this will show you video activity from social account you have connected to. Connecting to these sites will let YouTube send your activity to those other sites.

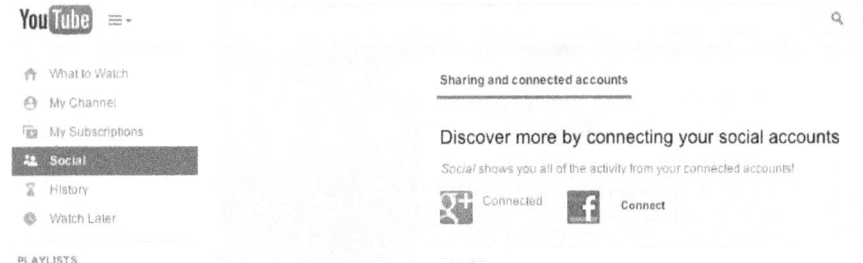

In this example, Google+ is the only social site connected. I will only see what people on my Google+ account have shared.

Under 'Social' is 'History'. Clicking this link shows you all of they videos you have watched in the past. You can choose to clear this history and whether you want the history to be public or private.

http://www.MarcBullard.com

Clicking 'Watch Later' takes you to that feed. This is where videos you have decided to watch at another time congregate until you view them.

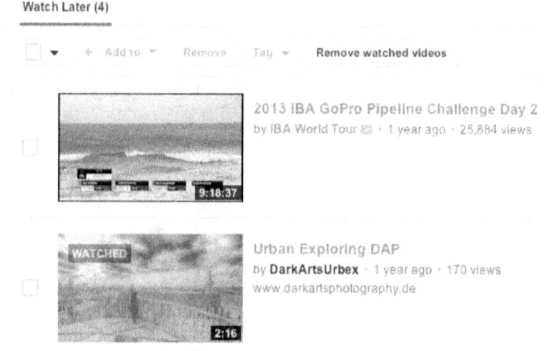

The next section on the left consists of Playlists. Clicking this red link will display the playlists you have created.

http://www.MarcBullard.com

PLAYLISTS

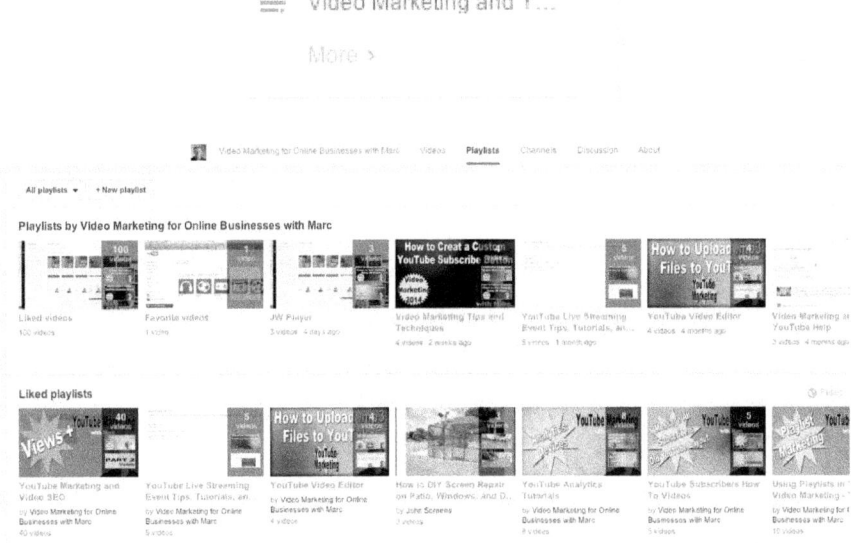

The next section is 'Subscriptions'. Clicking this red link will take you to the 'Manage Subscriptions' page.

'Manage subscriptions' allows you to change details about your subscriptions or to unsubscribe from any channel you are currently subscribed to. Here you can also choose to get emails whenever a specific channel uploads a new video. You also have the choice to only view upload information in your feed and not all of the other activity those users are doing.

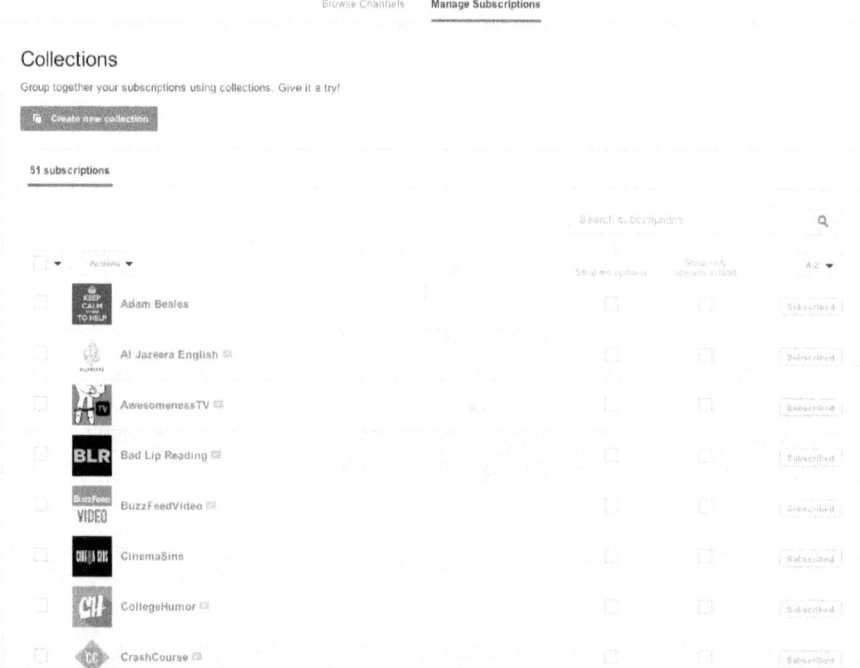

Below 'Subscriptions' on the left menu, is 'Browse channels'. If you click this, your feed will show popular categories and channels, some suggested to you based off of your viewing habits.

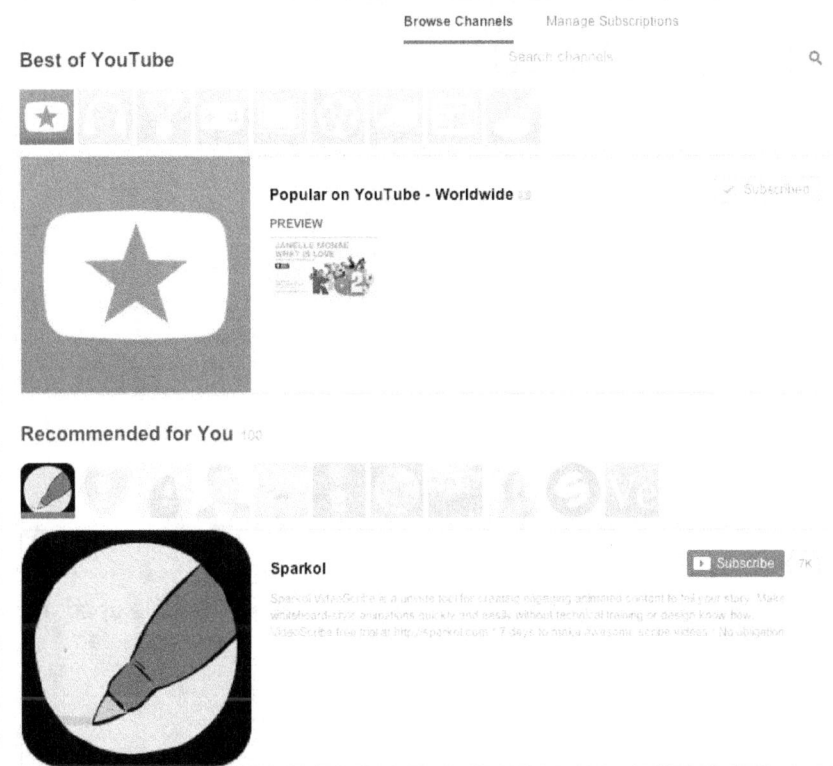

On the right hand side of your feed, you will see the 'Recommended Channels' column.

You can remove recommended channels by clicking the X in the upper right corner of each suggested channel. This will cause another suggested channel to appear.

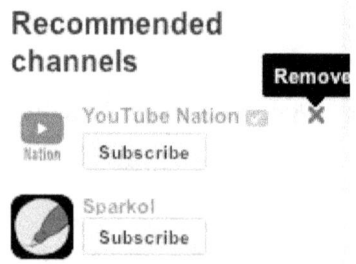

That's it for the home page. YouTube's goal is to keep this page clean and simplified. Now let's take a look at your user features.

User Features

In the far upper right area of YouTube is your username. Clicking this will bring up many more links.

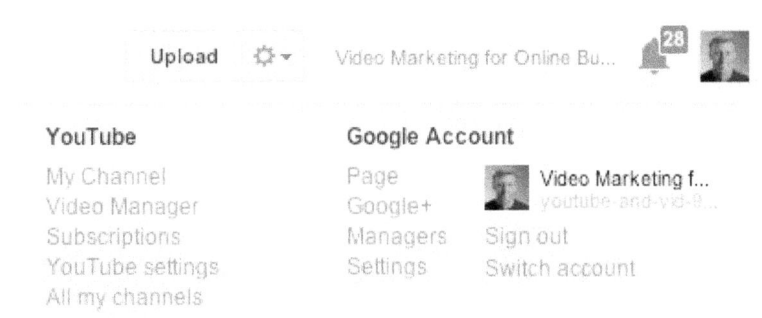

These links are broken down into 2 sections: YouTube and Google account. Google account contains links such as 'Profile/Page', 'Google+', 'Managers', etc. These links pertain to your Google account, not YouTube. The YouTube section contains links such as 'My channel', 'Video Manager', 'Subscriptions', 'YouTube settings' and 'All my channels'.

'My channel' will bring you to your YouTube channel.

http://www.MarcBullard.com

Your YouTube channel is very important for multiple reasons and will be discussed in more detail later. Additionally, you can access 'My Channel' by clicking the 'My Channel' link on the left guide.

In the upper right section under your username, the next link below 'My channel', is 'Video Manager'.

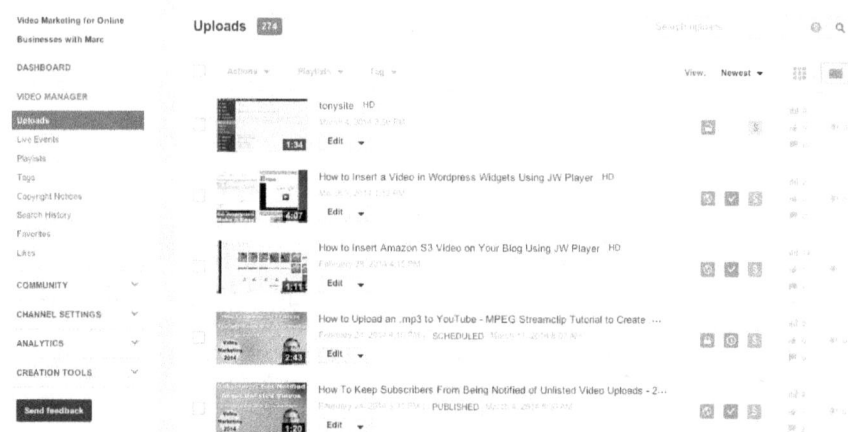

The 'Video Manager' is the behind-the-scenes cupboard that holds all of your uploaded videos. The middle feed area contains a thumbnail of your videos as well as edit options, view count, video accessibility and more.

Video Manager
On the left hand column of the Video Manager you have access to your 'Dashboard', 'Uploads', 'Live Events', 'Playlists', 'History', and more.

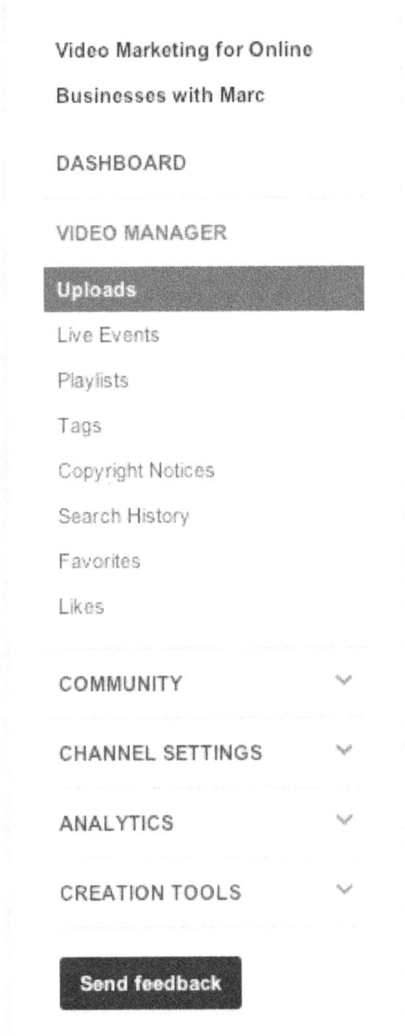

Video Marketing for Online

Businesses with Marc

DASHBOARD

VIDEO MANAGER

Uploads

Live Events

Playlists

Tags

Copyright Notices

Search History

Favorites

Likes

COMMUNITY ⌄

CHANNEL SETTINGS ⌄

ANALYTICS ⌄

CREATION TOOLS ⌄

Send feedback

The first link is the name of your channel. The link below that, 'Dashboard' contains general stats for your YouTube account such as uploaded videos, view counts, comments and more.

http://www.MarcBullard.com

Each small, squared section is known as a widget. Widgets can be added, removed, and rearranged to fit your needs. To add a widget, click the plus symbol and select what widget you want to add.

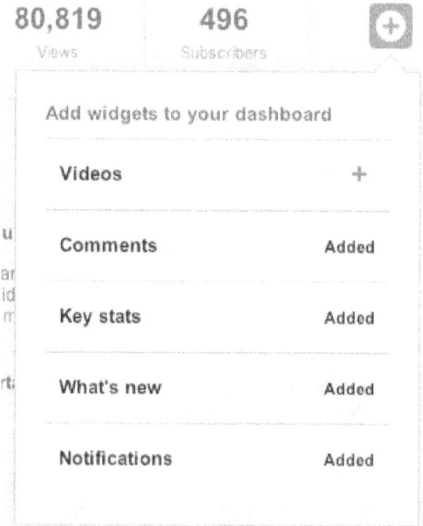

To remove or edit a widget, click the gear symbol in the upper right corner.

http://www.MarcBullard.com

MARC SWEET VIDEOS

This gear will provide you options to customize your widget. You can change the number of items shown, add a filter, and change the widget's name.

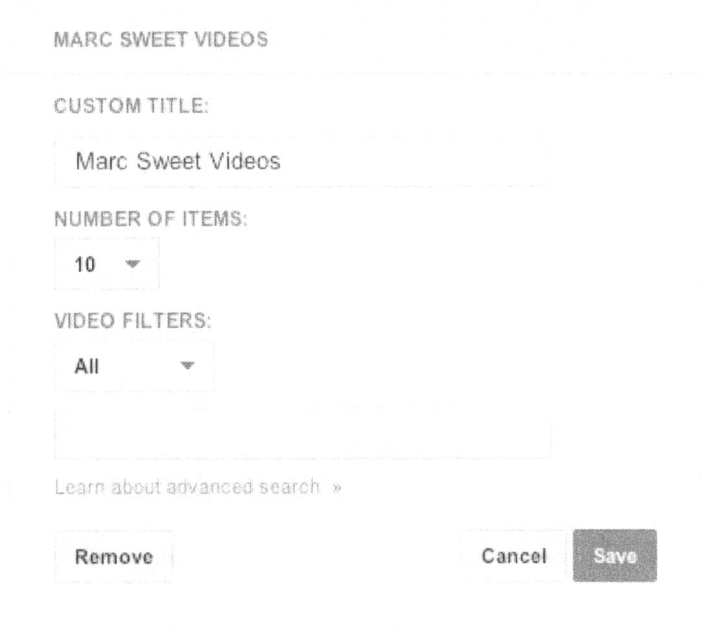

MARC SWEET VIDEOS

CUSTOM TITLE:

Marc Sweet Videos

NUMBER OF ITEMS:

10 ▼

VIDEO FILTERS:

All ▼

Learn about advanced search »

Remove   Cancel   Save

By clicking and dragging the 9 dots located next to the gear in each widget, you can move them into any order you wish.

The 'Uploads' link in the left hand column shows you a list of your uploaded videos.

http://www.MarcBullard.com

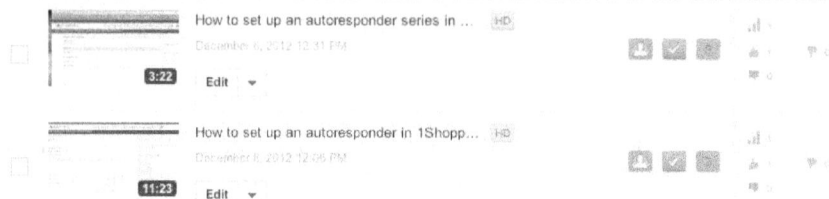

You also have options to Edit your video information and make enhancements, add annotations, add captions, download your file, and more.

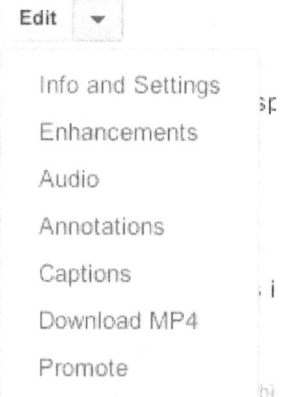

These options will be covered in more detail later.

The right hand side of each video contains information on whether your video is public, when it was published, whether it's monetized and viewing information.

The next link under 'Uploads' is 'Live Events'. 'Live Events' lets you stream live video right on to YouTube. This is an extremely powerful service that can be used for many different purposes. When you first go to 'Live Events' you will be taken to the Events page.

By default, this page will display any upcoming live events you have scheduled. There is also a dropdown box that lets you view Live now and Completed events.

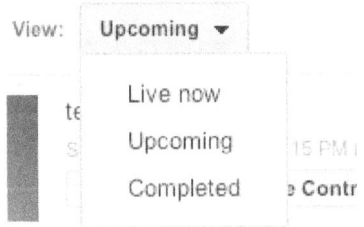

Upcoming events will show you the title and start date of the event as well as a thumbnail for that event. You will also have access to edit basic info and settings, Ingestion settings as well as access the Live Control Room.

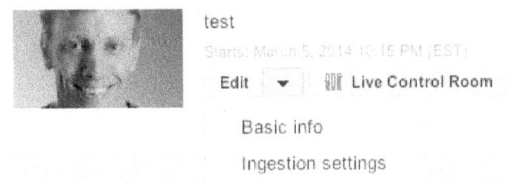

The upper right corner also has a button to create a new live event. When you create a new live event, you will be taken to the 'Info and Settings' page.

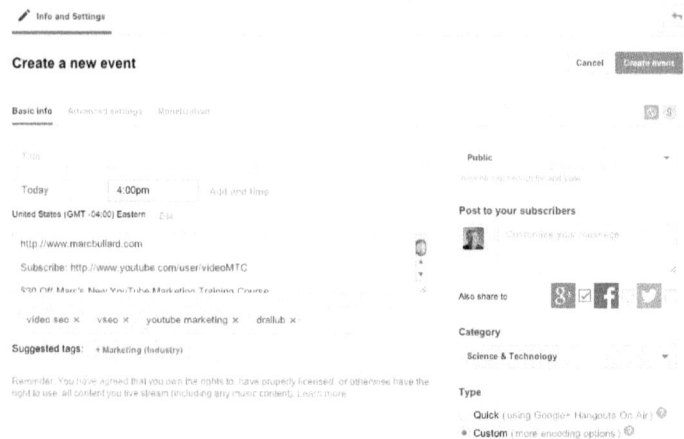

The 'Info and Settings' page has places to enter Title, start/end times, description, and tags. You can also set privacy access, post to subsribers, choose a category, share to social media sites, and determine what type of event you want it to be. This page also has tabs to access 'Advanced settings'.

http://www.MarcBullard.com

The 'Advanced settings' tab contains similar information as any other video in your video manager with a few differences. One difference is to let you decide how to promote your event.

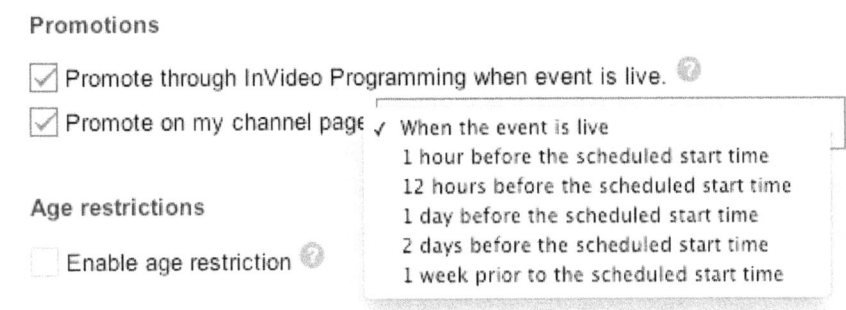

Promotions

Promote through InVideo Programming when event is live.

Promote on my channel page

✓ When the event is live
1 hour before the scheduled start time
12 hours before the scheduled start time
1 day before the scheduled start time
2 days before the scheduled start time
1 week prior to the scheduled start time

Age restrictions

Enable age restriction

You also have the choice to make the event private once it has ended, enable DVR, and broadcast delay.

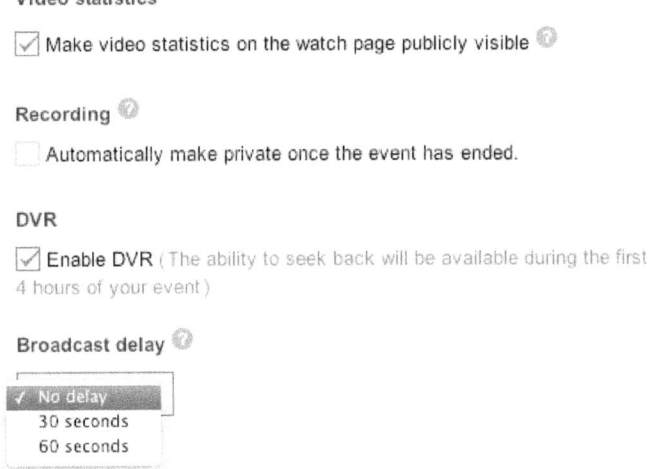

Video statistics

Make video statistics on the watch page publicly visible

Recording

Automatically make private once the event has ended.

DVR

Enable DVR (The ability to seek back will be available during the first 4 hours of your event)

Broadcast delay

✓ No delay
30 seconds
60 seconds

The 'Info and Settings' page also has a tab to let you monetize your live event if you choose to.

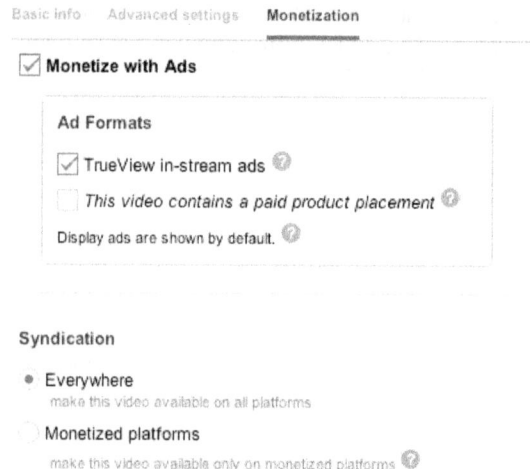

After you have finalized all of these settings, click the 'Create event' button. You will then be taken to the 'Ingestions settings' page.

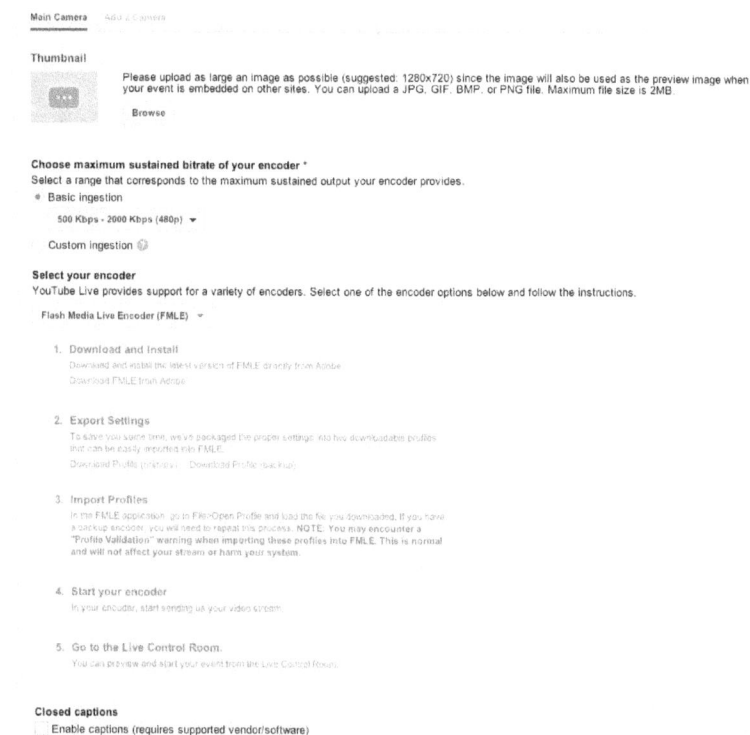

The first thing you will see on the 'Ingestion settings' page is for you to ad a camera and upload a customized thumbnail graphic for your event.

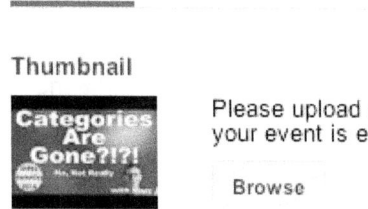

Upload a graphic that will help promote your event as well as let people know what it is about.

After that, the next choice is to set your maximum bitrate of your encoder.

Choose maximum sustained bitrate of your encoder *
Select a range that corresponds to the maximum sustained output your encoder provides.

• Basic ingestion

500 Kbps - 2000 Kbps (480p) ▼

3000 Kbps - 6000 Kbps (1080p)

1500 Kbps - 4000 Kbps (720p)

Sel

Yoι   500 Kbps - 2000 Kbps (480p)   of encoders. Select one of the encoder options ϧ

Fι   400 Kbps - 1000 Kbps (360p)

300 Kbps - 700 Kbps (240p)

Encoder settings are important to be aware of. If you look at the choices available, there are different Kbps (Kilobits per second) that your stream will be composed of. The higher the Kbps, the higher quality your stream will be (top 2 are HD). This also means that the higher it is, the more bandwidth you will need. If there is any lag in bandwidth you may not be able to stream your live video. You need to be sure to pick an option that you know will be compatible with your internet connection. Usually, to be on the safe side, I use 500Kbps – 2000Kbps. This setting has never been a problem when I stream. Another very important thing to remember is the number of cameras you have. If you have more than one camera, each additional camera takes up more bandwidth so you need to take that into consideration as well. There is also an option to set a custom stream that you can use on all of your live events.

Once you set your encoder settings, then next thing you need to do is select your encoder.

Select your encoder

Select an encoder   a val

Wirecast for YouTube

✓ Flash Media Live Encoder (FMLE)

Other encoders

Your encoder will take your video from your camera and create a file that can be streamed. The encoder can be a standalone box that your camera is plugged into and then linked to your computer, or you can use a software based encoder that is already on your computer. Examples of software based encoders are Wirecast for YouTube and Flash Media Live Encoder (FMLE).

Once you choose an encoder, the steps below will change to accommodate your selection.

1. Download and Install

   Download and install the latest version of FMLE directly from Adobe.

   Download FMLE from Adobe.

2. Export Settings

   To save you some time, we've packaged the proper settings into two downloadable profiles that can be easily imported into FMLE.

   Download Profile (primary)   Download Profile (backup)

3. Import Profiles

   In the FMLE application, go to File>Open Profile and load the file you downloaded. If you have a backup encoder, you will need to repeat this process. NOTE: You may encounter a "Profile Validation" warning when importing these profiles into FMLE. This is normal and will not affect your stream or harm your system.

4. Start your encoder

   In your encoder, start sending us your video stream.

5. Go to the Live Control Room.

   You can preview and start your event from the Live Control Room.

These are encoder steps if you choose Flash Media Live Encoder.

The next option is a check box you can use to enable captions.

Closed captions

☐ Enable captions (requires supported vendor/software)

Once you save your settings, you can go to the last tab, 'Live Control Room'.

The Live Control Room is for when you are ready to stream your event. It outlines the steps involved to start streaming.

test

Once you get your camera rolling (or screen capture software) and start your encoder of choice, you can click the 'Preview' button to see if everything is getting to YouTube. You will know if YouTube is getting your encoder's stream from the 'Stream Status' area.

STREAM STATUS

NO DATA

480P STREAM

AVERAGE LIVE VIEW
DURATION   00:00

TOTAL VIEW TIME (HOURS)   0

PEAK CONCURRENT   0

Below that, you can preview your stream to make sure everything is okay.

Below the preview window is an area for Broadcast Alerts, Slate Insertion,
Ads Insertion, and Highlights.

BROADCAST ALERT

✓ None
The broadcaster has cancelled this event.
The broadcaster has delayed the start of this event. Please try again later.
The broadcaster has ended this event early.
The broadcaster has rescheduled this event.
We are experiencing technical difficulties. Please try again later.

SLATES INSERTION

Slate in   Slate out

ADS INSERTION

Insert

In-stream ad insertion must be enabled for the live broadcast.

CREATE HIGHLIGHT

Set start   Set end   Upload

Highlights can only be created when "Sync to preview player" option is enabled.

Broadcast Alerts are messages that you can insert during the event to let viewers know if there is an issue.

Slates Insertion is used to show a graphic (slate) instead of your broadcast. This can be used for many purposes.

Ads Insertion is similar to slates, but instead of a graphic, YouTube will show an ad. Your live event must be public in order to insert ads.

Highlights are certain sections of your live stream that can be uploaded as a separate video. You set the start and end and then upload the highlight as. This is done during your live event and will appear as a separate video in your video manager.

http://www.MarcBullard.com

One more thing to be aware of in the Live Control Room is the button to view your stream on the actual page that others will view it. There is a button in the upper right that lets you access this page.

Once on the watch page, the player will let viewers know what the event status is.

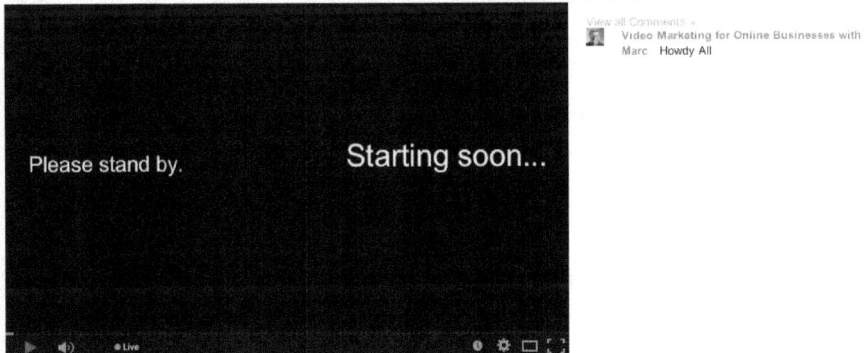

There is also an area for viewers to comment during your live stream. You can also establish moderators to reply to these comments.

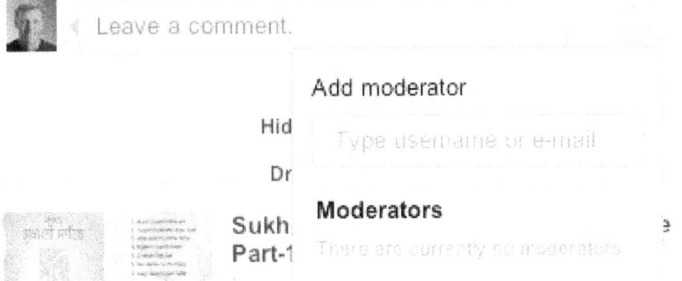

http://www.MarcBullard.com

Your YouTube Live Event is very similar to any other video on YouTube. You can even embed the video on your website so viewers can be directed there instead if you wish.

Back in the 'Video Manager' the 'Playlists' link below 'Uploads' displays playlists you have created.

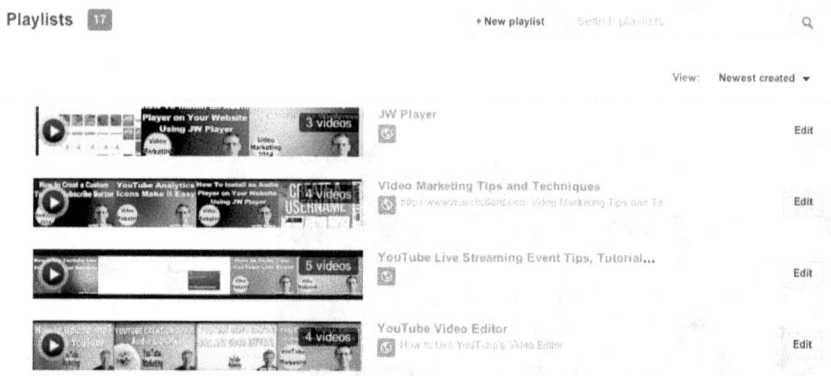

'Tags' shows you a list of tags that you have assigned your videos. You can use similar tags on multiple videos. This page lets you see what tags you've used and how many videos have that tag.

'Copyright Notices' shows you a list of videos that may have copyright issues with YouTube. You can get more information about these issues on the 'Copyright Notices' page.

http://www.MarcBullard.com

Copyright Notices

View: All ▾

Test 2. These are getting fun

Edit ▾ Video blocked in some countries.

Social Bookmarking Webinar - Social Bookmarking Power HD

Edit ▾ Matched third party content.

'Search History' provides a list of terms you have typed into YouTube's search bar. Just like viewing history, you can clear all of your search history or pause it.

My Search History

Remove | **Clear all search history** | **Pause search history**

lower thirds final cut
4 days ago

sdcard
1 week ago

'Favorites' provides information on videos that you have manually added to your favorites. You can also choose to play all or remove videos from your favorites.

http://www.MarcBullard.com

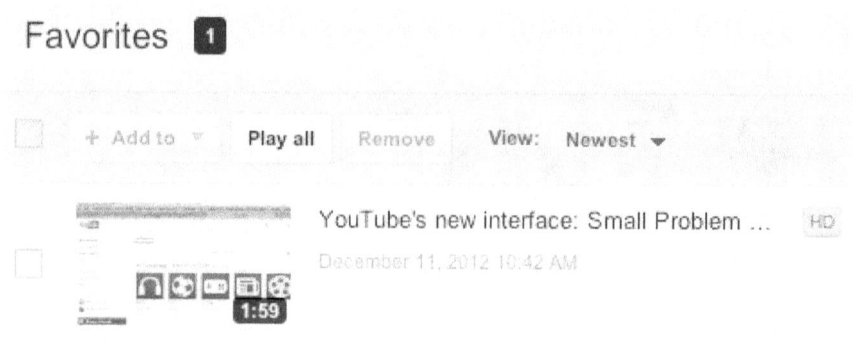

The 'Likes' link shows a list of your videos that you have voted a thumbs up for. Thumbs up indicates that you 'liked' that video.

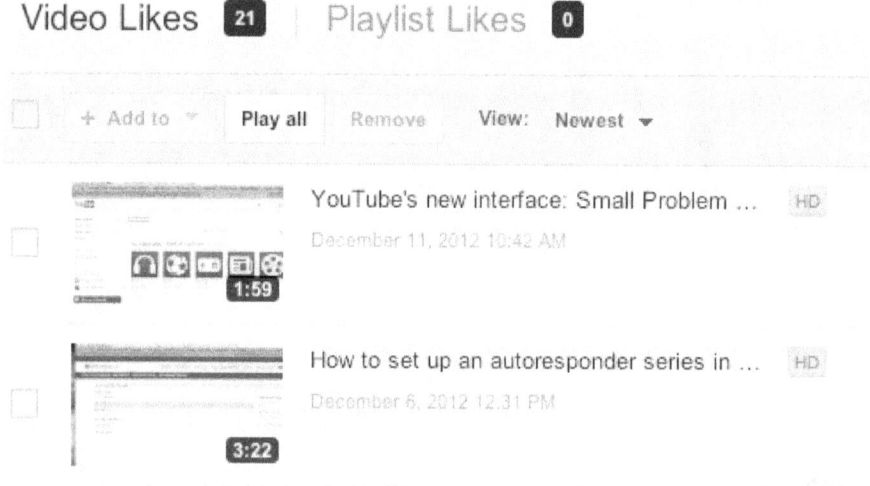

The Video Manager is a very important page on your account. You will be accessing this page often. There is also more than one way to access the Video Manager as well as other handy pages. Some of the other main pages in your account are easily found at the top of every page in your account.

http://www.MarcBullard.com

Under the 'Video Manager' options are more links to other handy pages. The next page is the 'Community' page.

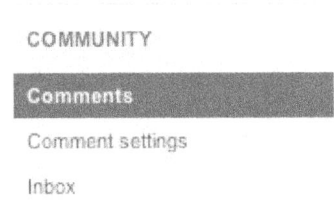

When you click 'Community', you will be taken to the 'Comments' section. The 'Comments' section is new for 2014. This is how all comments to your videos are viewed, approved, responded and deleted.

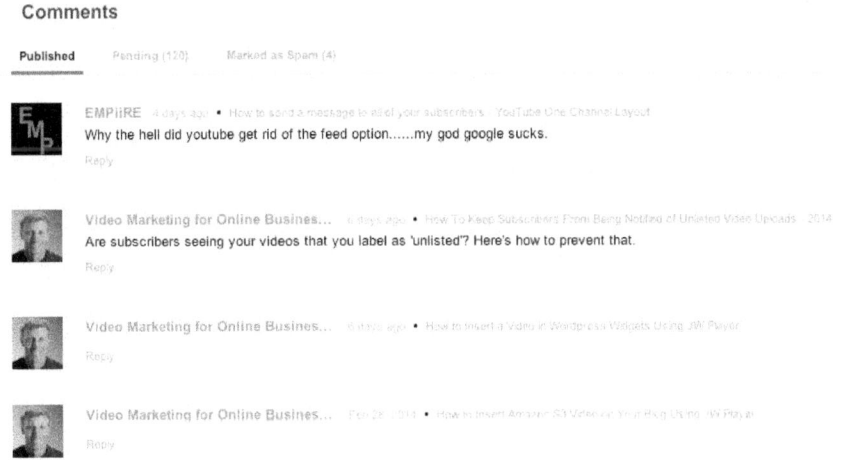

The 'Comments' page contains three tabs: 'Approved', 'Held for Review' and 'Likely Spam'.

Comments

Approved comments   **Held for review (42)**   Likely spam (1)

The 'Approved comments' tab is where you can view comments that are already visible to the public on YouTube. You can also reply to these comments as well as see what video it was that the comment is on.

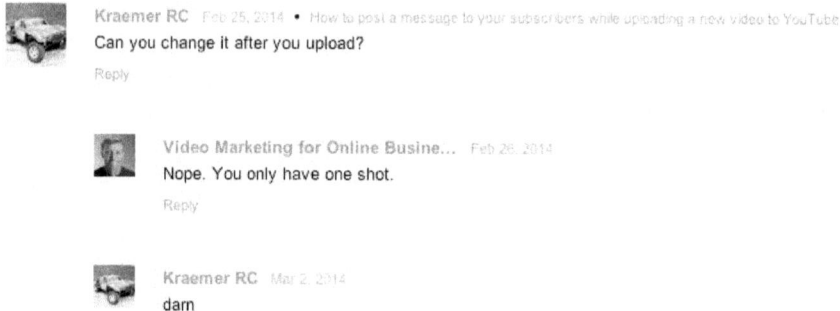

The next tab, 'Held for review' has all of the comments that are waiting for you to approve, remove, or report as spam.

You can also approve, remove, or mark as spam in bulk by selecting the check box next to those videos and selecting the corresponding button.

http://www.MarcBullard.com

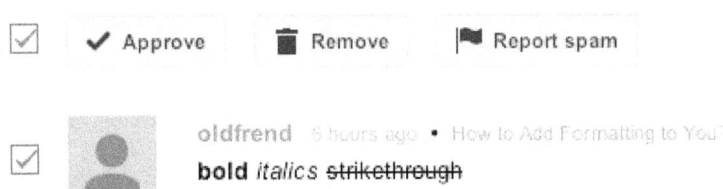

The 'Likely Spam' tab is very similar to the 'Held for review' tab. You can choose to approve, remove or flag these comments.

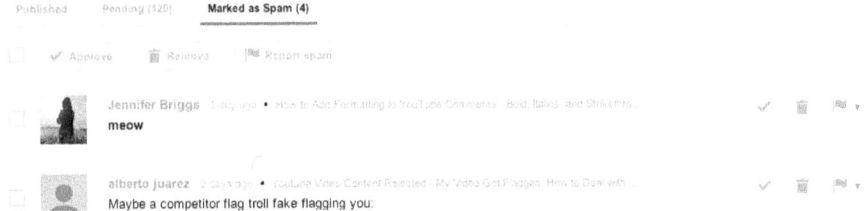

Another interesting option on both the 'Approved comments' and 'Likey Spam' tabs is the flag option. You have two choices: Report spam or Ban from channel. Report spam will alert YouTube and Ban from channel will keep that specific username from leaving any comments on your channel.

The next link under the 'Community' section is for 'Comment settings'. This page will let you set filters for your comments. These include Approved users, Banned users, and Blacklist.

http://www.MarcBullard.com

Comment settings

Automated filters

These filters apply to **new comments on your channel and videos**. Learn more

Approved users
Always show comments from these users.

+ Add names, circles, or email addresses

Banned users
Never show comments from these users.

+ Add names, circles, or email addresses

Blacklist
Comments closely matching these words will
be held for review.

viagra, cialis,

Default settings

On your new videos

○ Allow all comments
● Hold all comments for review
○ Disable comments

On your channel

○ Allow all comments
● Hold all comments for review
○ Disable comments

Approved users is where you can manually add users – by name, Google+ circles, or email address. These users' comments will always be approved. Banned users acts the same. Enter in a name, Google+ circle, or email address and those users' comments will never be approved/shown. Blacklist is a list of words you manually enter. Any comments that contain any of these words will be held for review.

You can also set default settings for comments.

http://www.MarcBullard.com

Default settings

On your new videos

○ Allow all comments

● Hold all comments for review

○ Disable comments

On your channel

○ Allow all comments

● Hold all comments for review

○ Disable comments

The default settings let you choose how to handle comments on new videos and well as comments on your channel. Your choices are: 'Allow all comments', 'Hold all comments for review', and 'Disable comments.

'Inbox is the last link under 'Community'. The 'Inbox' is similar to any mail program's inbox. This is where users can send you private messages. The left sidebar area lets you see messages broken down into different categories. You can also view messages you have sent as well as an address book of your contacts.

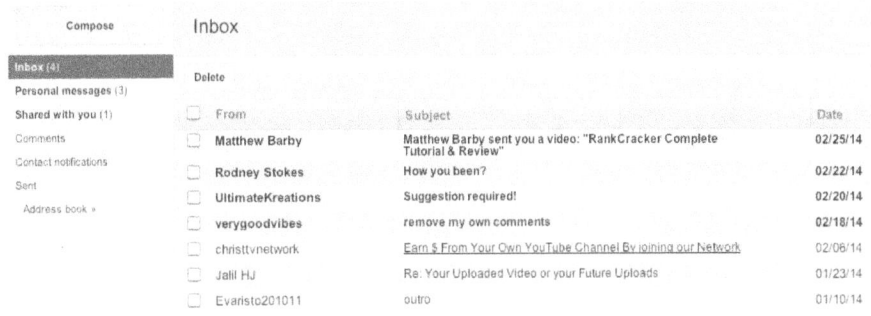

The Address Book lets you view and add contacts, compose messages, and block or delete certain users.

http://www.MarcBullard.com

New ▾

All Contacts

All Contacts (17)

Blocked Users (3)

Subscribers

Subscriptions

Add New   Compose   Block   Delete

☐ | Name ↓

Selected Contacts (0)

☐ Pudd Lane
☐ BigVisionShow
☐ FERMENTAS30
☐ INFO Wars Boot Camp
☐ LearnClassicalGuitar
☐ Adam Beales
☐ Video IoeKnows

Choose from your list of contacts

Under 'Community' is the link to 'Channel Settings'. Clicking this will bring you to your Features page.

The Features page provides information on your account status as well as additional features that YouTube may provide you such as: monetization, unlimited uploads, custom thumbnails, and more.

Features

To enable these features, your account must be in good standing.

Account status

Video Marketing for Online Businesses with Marc	**Partner Verified**
Community guidelines	Good standing
Copyright strikes	Good standing
Content ID claims	Good standing

Feature	Status	Description
Monetization		You can use ads to monetize your videos. View monetization settings
Longer videos		You can now upload videos longer than 15 minutes! Learn more
External annotations		Lets you link annotations to external sites or merch partners. Learn more
Custom thumbnails		Choose your video's thumbnail by uploading your own. Learn more
Paid Subscriptions		You must have at least 10.000 existing subscribers to enable this feature. Learn more
Content ID appeals		Lets you appeal rejected Content ID disputes. Learn more

Features page on new YouTube account

Depending on your account status, you might see a 'Verify' button as well as some of these options that need to be enabled.

http://www.MarcBullard.com

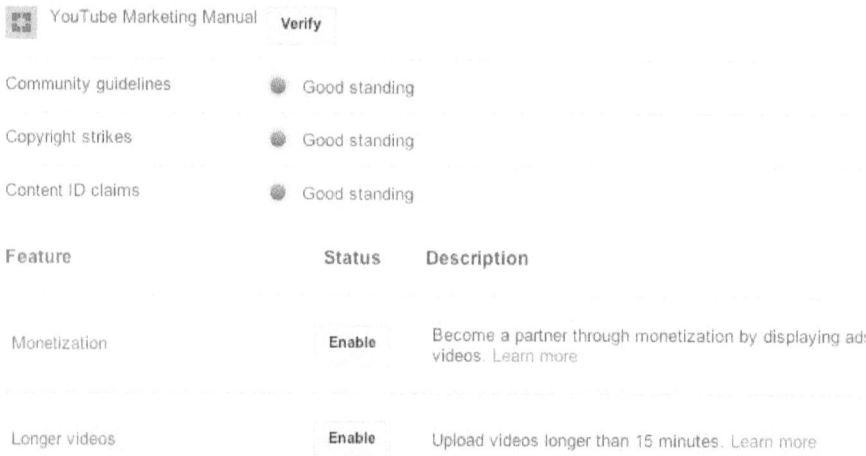

It is a good idea to enable as many of these as you can and verify your account. Verifying your account by phone lets you unlock additional features on YouTube.

Verifying your account is simple. Click the 'Verify' button. This will take you to a 2 step process. First, YouTube asks for a phone number to see if you're a real person.

Select your country

United States ▾

How should we deliver the verification code to you?

○ Call me with an automated voice message

● Text me the verification code

Which language should we use to send you the verification code?
English (US) change language

What is your phone number?

For example: (201) 555-5555

Choose whether you want a text message or voice recorded message. YouTube will text/call you with a code.

Verify Your YouTube Account

Account Verification (Step 2 of 2)

Your code has been sent to ███████ Please enter it below to complete the verification.

ENTER YOUR CODE

Verify

Enter the code and click the 'Verify' button. That's it, you're done.

Under the list of features, you will see options for monetization, longer videos, and more. Monetization is first. To be considered a YouTube partner and access promotional and skill-building opportunities, you must have at least one video approved for monetization. Click the 'Enable' button.

The Monetization page shows if you have that option turned on. Here you can choose to monetize all of your videos at once or you can choose to only monetize a select few. This page also lets you disable monetization as well as provides information and guidelines.

Monetization

Account Status

Your account is not enabled for monetization. Enabling your account allows you to monetize your videos.

Having at least one video approved for monetization makes you a YouTube partner, which provides you with opportunities to improve your skills and build your audiences. Learn more about the benefits of becoming a YouTube partner.

Enable My Account

Guidelines and Information

▼ **How can my videos make money?**

Once your video is submitted and approved for monetization, YouTube will place ads inside or near the video. After you've associated an AdSense account with your YouTube account, you will earn revenue that is generated from the ads. Learn more

▼ **How much will my videos earn?**

Earnings will depend on a number of factors. The two key factors are the type of ads and the pricing of ads appearing with your videos.

▼ **What types of videos are eligible?**

For a video to be eligible, you must own worldwide commercial usage rights to everything in the video and the video must abide by our Terms of Service and Community Guidelines.

This means you have created everything in your video yourself, and you did not sell exclusive commercial usage rights to someone else. If your video contains content created by someone else, you must have their written permission to use and make money from it.

You may also share in the monetization of eligible cover videos. Learn more

Examples of videos that could be eligible include:

You filmed your cat and there is no background music.
Your video contains royalty-free music, and you can prove commercial rights using direct links to the song and applicable license.
Your friend's band wrote and recorded a song for your video and states in writing that you can use and make money from it.

The next feature you can enable is for uploading longer videos. By default, you can upload videos up to 15 minutes. If you want to upload videos longer than that, enable this feature. In order to upload longer videos, you'll need to verify your account.

Longer videos   **Enable**   Upload videos longer than 15 minutes. Learn more

After longer videos, you have the option to enable External annotations.

External annotations   ●   Lets you link annotations to external sites or merch partners. Learn more

External annotations are extremely important for your YouTube channel as well as for your website. YouTube only let's you put a link that exits YouTube in three places. This is one of those three places. As long as your account is verified and in good standing, you qualify for external annotations. You definitely want to enable this feature. External annotations will be covered in more detail later in this book.

Custom thumbnails is the next feature available. You do want this enabled. Custom thumbnails help brand your videos and is known to improve your search rankings in YouTube.

Paid Subscriptions will probably 'greyed out' for most accounts. This feature is for very popular YouTube channels that have at least 10,000 subscribers (not to say you can't get there with your channel). This feature lets YouTube channels charge people to see their content.

Content ID appeals is good if you need to claim video content is yours. You may need to do this if somebody copied your video/music and put it elsewhere on YouTube. As long as your account is in good standing and verified, you will have this feature enabled.

Unlisted and private videos will be enabled as long as your account is in good standing.

Live events lets you stream live video directly over YouTube. As long as your account is in good standing, you will have this enabled.

On the left menu under 'Channel Settings', there are additional links. Monetization, Defaults, and more. Monetization will take you to the same page as before. The next option below Monetization is 'Defaults'.

CHANNEL SETTINGS

Features

Monetization

Defaults

InVideo Programming

Fan Finder

Advanced

'Defaults' let you set certain parameters that will apply to every uploaded video. You can choose the privacy level, categories, title, description, tags, and more. You can also edit this information for individual videos through the video manager. Using this feature is very handy and will speed up your marketing efforts.

Under 'Defaults' on the left menu is 'InVideo Programming'. This is a nice feature that gives you the power to brand your channel on all of your videos. It acts like a picture annotation in the fact that it shows up on the screen and viewers can click on it. When they click the image, it either takes them to your channel or a specific video; you decide. You can also pick where on the screen it is located and when it should appear on the screen.

InVideo Programming

Drive viewership to a specific video and reinforce channel branding using InVideo Programming across all your videos

Featured Channel

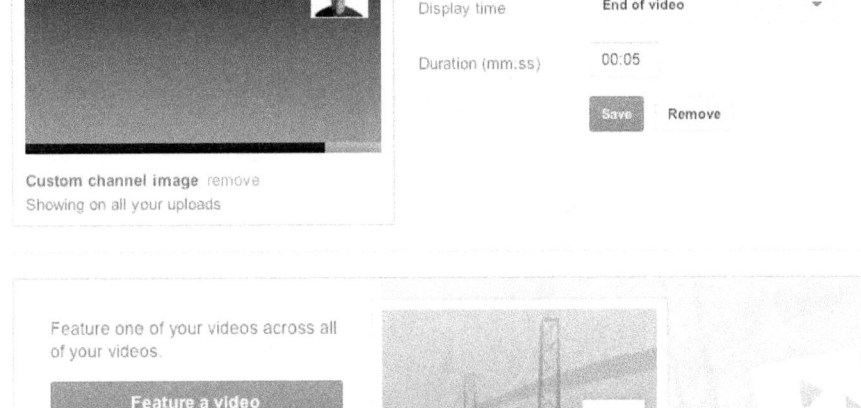

You can track all your InVideo Programming campaigns by downloading the report. Download

The next link on the left menu is for 'Fan Finder'. Fan Finder is a feature to let YouTube promote your channel to the people most likely to love your videos. It's simply a trailer video to promote your YouTube channel. This feature will be discussed in more detail in the marketing section of this book.

http://www.MarcBullard.com

Fan Finder

Find more fans by letting YouTube promote your channel to the people most likely to love your videos Fan Finder and get started.

Explore channel ad tips and best practices. Learn more

Select your channel ad

The last link under 'Channel Settings' is 'Advanced'. The 'Advanced' page contains account information as well as other settings you can use to customize your YouTube channel.

Account Information

Video Marketing for Online Businesses with Marc change

change

Country	United States	▼

Channel keywords	"online video" "video marketing" "online bus

Advertisements

● Allow advertisements to be displayed alongside my videos

○ Do not allow advertisements to be displayed alongside my videos

Ads will only be displayed for videos where you own all the rights. Choosing this option will disable any monetization options that have been set for your videos.

The first thing you see in the middle of the page is Account Information. This shows you the name of your channel, your Icon image, your country, and channel keywords. It's a good idea to name your channel with relevant keywords. You can change the name of your channel by clicking the 'change' link. Make sure you put relevant keywords in the Channel keywords box. More information about keywords is later in this book.

Below Account information is Advertisements. You have two choices: allow advertisements or do not allow advertisements. It is recommended that you choose to allow advertisements because if you turn them off, then your monetization is disabled.

The next section is to link an Adwords account.

Link an AdWords for video account

Linking your YouTube channel to an AdWords for video account allows you to promote your video and access reporting.

Link an AdWords account

Account name	Customer ID	Permissions	Options

http://www.MarcBullard.com

If you monetize and want to get paid from the ads that are on your videos, you will need to link an adwords account to this channel.

The next section is for an Associated Website. This is extremely important for marketing on YouTube. The Associated Website page gives you the option to tell YouTube of any website you're associated with. This helps improve the quality of YouTube's search results and helps brand you or your business. The process to connect your website to YouTube is fairly simple yet it does consist of logging into your web host and uploading a file.

Associated Website

Tell us if your channel is associated with another website. This will help us improve the quality of our search results and verify your channel as the official representation of your brand on YouTube.

Your Website:

Success   Remove

To associate a website with your YouTube channel, first type the domain name into the Your Website box. Then click the 'Add' button.

http://www.mysite.com| Add

After clicking 'Add', you will see a status of Pending.

Pending   Refresh   Remove

You can request approval from the website owner or if you own the site, verify that you own it.

You can then request approval from the website owner or if you own the site, verify it. Let's assume this is for your own site. Clicking the verify link will take you to Webmaster Central. On this page are directions on how to add a tag to your home page.

Verify your ownership of **http://www.mysite.com/**. Learn more.

Recommended method   Alternate methods

Recommended: HTML tag

Add a meta tag to your site's home page.

1. Copy the meta tag below, and paste it into your site's home page. It should go in the <head> section, before the first <body> section.

<meta name="google-site-verificatio

▶ Show me an example

2. Click **Verify** below.

To stay verified, don't remove the meta tag, even after verification succeeds.

There are alternative methods to verifying ownership of you website too.

Recommended method   **Alternate methods**

○ **HTML file upload**
Upload an HTML file to your site.

○ **Domain name provider**
Sign in to your domain name provider.

○ **Google Analytics**
Use your Google Analytics account.

○ **Google Tag Manager**
Use your Google Tag Manager account.

VERIFY   Not now

Once you have done one of these methods, click the 'Verify' button. You will know you're successful if the status of your associated website is green.

http://www.MarcBullard.com

Associated website

Tell us if your channel is associated with another website. This will help us improve the quality of our search results and verify your channel as the official representation of your brand on YouTube.

⬤ Success | **Remove**

The next section under Associated website is for Channel recommendations. There are two options. You want to allow the channel to appear in other recommendations. This will help you get found by others.

Channel recommendations

⦿ Allow my channel to appear in other channels' recommendations

◯ Do not allow my channel to appear in other channels' recommendations

Subscriber Counts

⦿ Display the number of people subscribed to my channel

◯ Do not display the number of people subscribed to my channel

Google Analytics account ID

The next section is for Subscriber Counts. You can choose to display or not display the number of people subscribed. This doesn't hurt you with search rankings if you turn it off or leave it on. If you are just starting out you may have only a few subscribers so you may want to not display for the time being.

Below that is an area to enter a Google Analytics account ID. This can give you interesting information about who is visiting your YouTube channel.

http://www.MarcBullard.com

The next link in the left menu is for 'Analytics'.

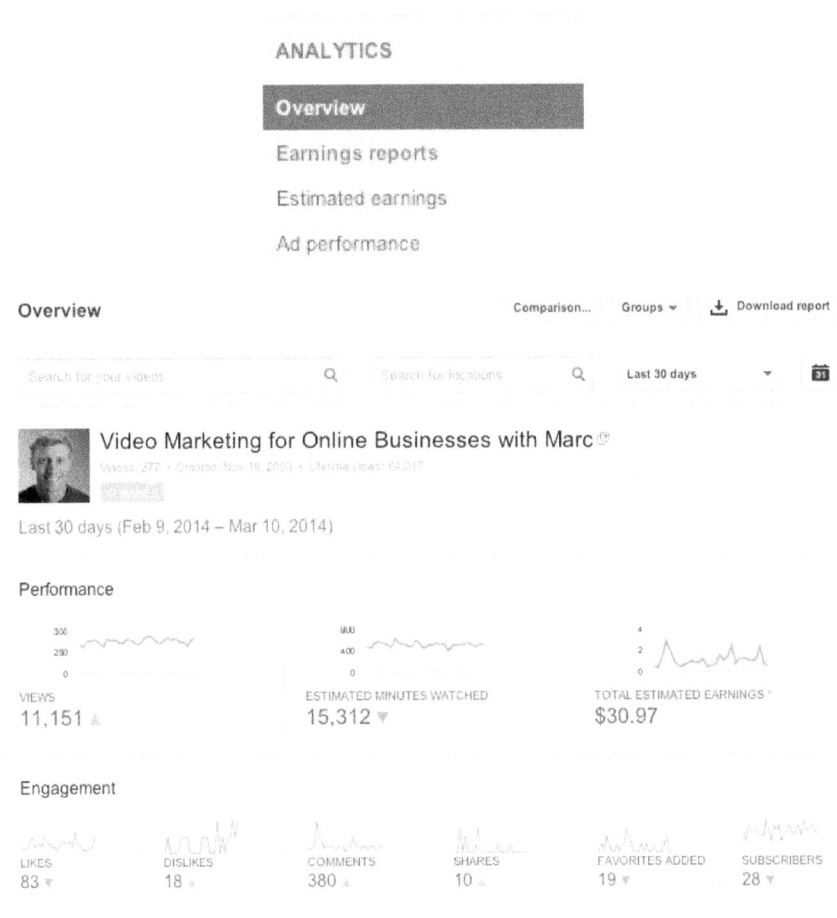

Analytics is a complex tool to provide you information on your videos, such as view counts, minutes watched, demographics and more. A detailed write up on how to use Analytics is in the Analytics section of this book.

http://www.MarcBullard.com

The next link under 'Analytics' is 'Creation Tools'.

CREATION TOOLS

Audio Library

Video Editor

'Creation Tools' consists of two links: 'Audio Library' and 'Video Editor'. More detail on the 'Video Editor' will be in the 'Video Editor' section of this book. 'Audio Tools' is an audio library that contains royalty free music.

Audio Library

Download background music for your videos. For **free**.

Featured	Genre	Mood	Instrument	Duration	Favorites	Q			
▶ Moonlight Sonata (by Beethoven)				5:18	Beethoven	Classical | Dark		⬇	★
▶ The Engagement				2:27	Silent Partner	Country & Folk | Romantic		⬇	★
▶ Tidal Wave				2:06	Silent Partner	Alternative & Punk | Happy		⬇	★
▶ Standing Here				2:52	Silent Partner	Hip Hop & Rap | Romantic		⬇	★
▶ Strange Ways				3:33	Silent Partner	Ambient | Dark		⬇	★
▶ Gotta Find Out				2:30	Silent Partner	R&B & Soul | Calm		⬇	★
▶ Daisy Dukes				2:57	Silent Partner	Country & Folk | Dark		⬇	★
▶ Drop and Roll				2:02	Silent Partner	Rock | Angry		⬇	★
▶ The Messenger				2:12	Silent Partner	Jazz & Blues | Happy		⬇	★
▶ Fortaleza				3:00	Topher Mohr and Alex ...	Jazz & Blues | Calm		⬇	★

Terms and conditions   Interested in seeing your tracks in this library? Let us know.

http://www.MarcBullard.com

This royalty free music can be downloaded and used in your videos for free. The music can be broken down by genre, mood, instrument and more.

Featured   Genre   Mood   Instrument   Duration   Favorites

If you find a track that you want to use, simply click the download button and save it to your computer. You can now use this song when you edit your video.

That's it for all of the available links in this section. If you remember, we accessed all of this by clicking the username in the upper right hand corner, which provided us links such as Channel and Video Manager.

YouTube

My Channel
Video Manager
Subscriptions
YouTube settings
All my channels

Google Account

Page
Google+
Managers
Settings

Video Marketing f...
youtube-and-vid-9...
Sign out
Switch account

There are still more links located under the username.

The next link under your YouTube links is 'Subscriptions'. This is the same as accessing 'My Subscriptions' from the Guide. Clicking this 'Subscriptions' link will take you to your 'My Subscriptions' page.

The last link in your username is for 'YouTube Settings'. The 'YouTube Settings' page provides you with a lot of options to customize your account.

Overview

Account information

Name   Video Marketing for Online Businesses with Marc   Edit on Google+
                                       Advanced

Mobile uploads   edhjky9v99jx@m.youtube.com
                         Upload videos from your phone by emailing this address. Want a different address? Click Here

Managers   Add or remove managers
                         You will be redirected to the Google+ managers page

Additional features

View additional features
See all my channels or create a new channel

The first section you will come to is Overview. Overview gives you options to view and change account information, get a mobile upload link, add or remove managers, view additional features, see all of your channels, and create a new channel.

The left sidebar shows you other account settings such as: Connected accounts, Privacy, Email, Playback, and Connected TVs.

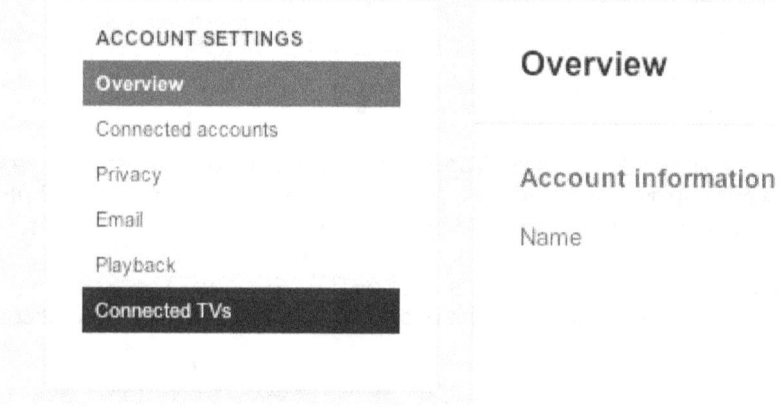

On the Overview page, under your username, you will see an 'Advanced' link. If you click this link it will take you to a page that you can change your password, delete your channel, and more.

The next link on the left hand menu is to access 'Connected accounts'.

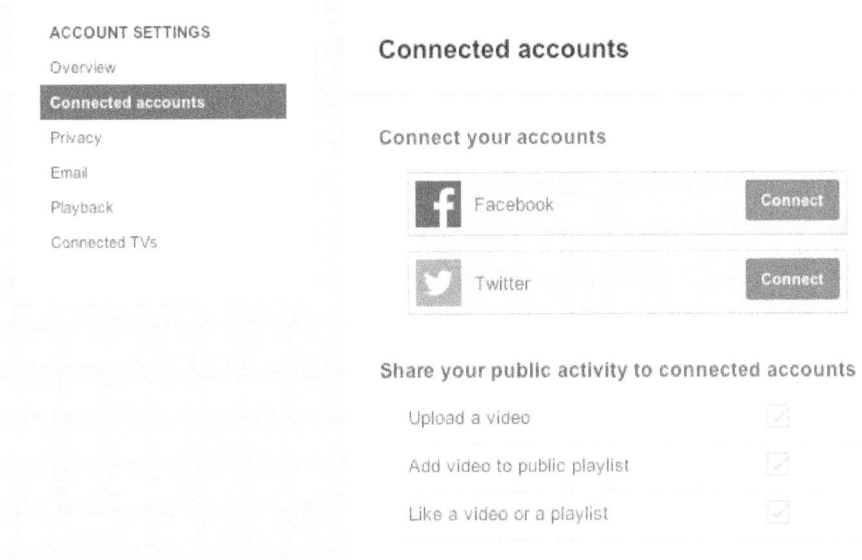

Here you can connect your other social networking sites to your YouTube channel. You can also determine how much activity you want shared on these accounts.

The 'Privacy' page lets you determine what you want others to know about your YouTube activity.

ACCOUNT SETTINGS

Overview

Connected accounts

Privacy

Email

Playback

Connected TVs

Privacy

Likes and Subscriptions

☐ Keep all my Liked Videos and Liked Playlists private

☐ Keep all my subscriptions private

Search and contacts

☐ Allow **only my contacts** to send me messages and share videos

Ads based on my interest

We try to serve you relevant ads based on your online browsing behavi settings from your Google Ads Settings. From there, you can do the fo

- view or manage your demographics and interest categories
- block certain advertisers
- opt out of interest-based ads

The Email page lets you change your email information. You can also subscribe/unsubscribe to email notifications and newsletters.

Email address

Google+ Page notification email

Emails about your subscriptions

Send me the YouTube wrap-up, a summary of the latest activity on my subscriptions: **Once a week** ▼

Also send me emails when:

☑ A YouTube Live Event is starting soon
☑ I subscribe to new channels

New uploads: Get emailed right when your favorite channels upload new videos. Edit settings

Emails about your channel, your videos and your comments

Email settings for notifications about comments on your videos or your channel, as well as replies to your comments can be changed by visiting Google+ notification settings.

Send me emails when:

☑ Someone subscribes to my channel
☑ Someone leaves a comment on my private video or responds to my comments on a private video
☑ I receive a private message or a shared video
☐ My video upload is complete

YouTube Newsletters

Select which occasional product related newsletters you would like to receive from YouTube:

☑ All YouTube newsletters
☑ General updates (including YouTube Broadcast)
☑ Popular on YouTube

Language

Your email language is **English (US)** ▼

Don't want email from YouTube?

☐ Do not send me any emails

Playback gives you viewing options. Here, you can choose what quality you want to view your videos with and whether annotations and captions are seen or not.

Playback

Video playback quality

- ● Always choose the best quality for my connection and player size
  - ☐ Always play HD on fullscreen (when available)
- ○ I have a slow connection. Never play higher-quality video

Annotations

- ☑ Show annotations on videos

Captions

- ☑ Always show captions
- ☐ Show automatic captions by speech recognition (when available)

The last link is for 'Connected TVs'. Use this page to connect your TV to YouTube. Once your TV is connected, you will then be able to choose where you watch YouTube.

Uploading and Video Optimization

Uploading your video is the first step in the YouTube marketing process. YouTube makes it fairly simple to upload and provide information to any video. The information you provide is extremely important when it comes to search engine positioning – YouTube's search engine as well as Google.

Once logged in, you will see an 'Upload' button located at the top right of the site. Accompanying this button is an arrow that drops down more choices: 'Dashboard,'Video Manager', 'Analytics', 'YouTube settings, and help.

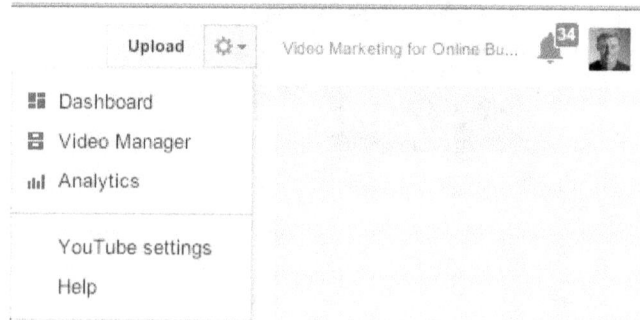

After clicking the 'Upload' button, you will be directed to the 'Upload video files' page.

CREATE VIDEOS

Webcam capture
Record

Photo slideshow
Create

Google+ Hangouts
On Air
Broadcast

Video editor
Edit

Select files to upload

Or drag and drop video files

Public ▾

This page lets you select files to upload as well as options to create a video by recording with a webcam, create a photo slideshow, or create a live video broadcast via Google+ hangouts On Air. You can also access the Video editor from this page. Most of the time you will be uploading files that are on your computer. Click 'Select files to upload' and then select the file from your computer that you want to upload.

After you select your video file, the 'Uploading' page will appear. This page contains a progress bar, some tabs, and areas to enter Title, Description, and Tags. You can also set privacy settings, post to your subscribers, share options, and choose a category.

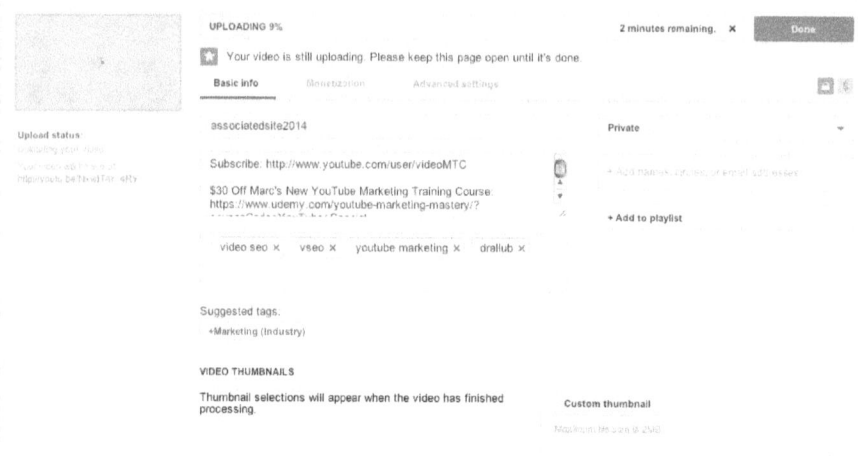

Uploading your video is one thing, optimizing your video is another. Optimizing your video information is going to make the difference between getting found on YouTube and Google or not. There's many ways to optimize your videos, but the three most powerful are optimizing your title, description, and tags.

Title

The title is extremely important. It's one of the first things Youtube and viewers see in Youtube's search results. It also shows up in Google results. Putting keywords in your YouTube title is the first of many things you should do to your uploaded videos. Keywords are words or phrases that the average web surfer would type into a search box in order to get more information on whatever subject they are interested in. Every business has certain keywords related to them, for example: An online health food store would want to get people looking for 'organic', 'vegan', or 'omega-3' as these are words that are being typed into Google by the health food store's potential customer.

http://www.MarcBullard.com

Now let's say there were two online health food stores. Store 1 makes a video that talks about all of the benefits of some new vitamins. When it comes time to enter in the title, they put 'Check out these new vitamins'. Store 2 also makes a video about the same vitamins but they put in the title box 'Vegan Vitamins - Daily Dose of Omega-3s'.

The second store's video will be seen by a lot more people. Not only that, the people going to see Store 2's video are going to be a more targeted niche, particularly those who are interested in either 'vegan' things, 'omega-3s' or both. You can now cater to that niche more exclusively.

I do have a word of warning about the above example. When you title your videos, they must be related to what the video is about. If Store 2 had used that title but the vitamins didn't have any of those benefits, people will click away, possibly losing a potential customer or sale. Nobody likes to be tricked. Be sure to be truthful in your titles. Not only that, YouTube lets viewers 'Flag' videos. To 'Flag' a video means that YouTube now knows your video didn't sit right with that viewer for whatever reason. If the video gets 'Flagged' too much, YouTube may take down that video or even disable your account.

The dreaded 'Flag'

Just so you know, be sure to put the most valuable keywords closest to the beginning of the title. For example, if your video is about YouTube

Marketing, you want to try to put the phrase 'YouTube Marketing' near the beginning. The title would have more search engine value if you title it 'YouTube Marketing – Put Keywords in your title' compared to 'Want to Learn YouTube Marketing?'

For unknown reasons YouTube/Google will sometimes give preference to videos that have the primary keyword first and then the link right after it. So let's see what it looks like.

Option 1 – http://www.mydomain.com – My keyword phrase the rest of my description.

Option 2 – My keyword phrase – http://www.mydomain.com the rest of my description.

Try out both methods. Using Analytics will help you narrow in on the best way to title your video.

How to find keywords
Finding keywords is one of the most important jobs you have to do. Using the right keywords means the difference between nobody finding your video and everybody finding it. Since this is a book on video marketing, I'm not going to go into too much detail about keyword research but it does need to be discussed.

There are many free keyword tools online, some better than others. There are also pay versions with many more options to choose from. One of the best and free keyword tools out there is Wordtracker's Free Keyword Tool. freekeywords.wordtracker.com

Once you go to the site, type in an example of a phrase that your audience might be interested in, for example: Pets.

Find Keywords

After you type in the phrase in the keyword box, choose to search in US or globally and how you want to match the keywords. Then, click the 'Search' button.

Once the results show up, you will have a list of similar keywords you might want to use in your videos. In order to determine if it's a keyword worth using, take a look at the 'Searches' column. The higher the number, the better. You also want to be mindful of the competition. The lower the competition the easier it will be for you to show up in search results. Keywords with large Global Monthly Searches as well as low competition are some of the best to work with.

There are many more detailed write-ups on finding keywords. This is just a basic summary of how to get started. For more information, be sure to do your research.

http://www.MarcBullard.com

YouTube Keyword Suggestion Tool - https://ads.youtube.com/keyword_tool

YouTube now provides you with a keyword suggestion tool all of their own. The Keyword Suggestion Tool searches only within YouTube so your results are different than Google's.

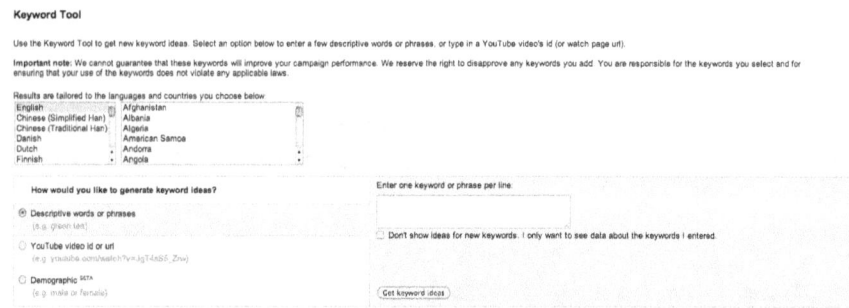

Other than choosing a language and country that keywords are tailored to, YouTube's keyword suggestion tool consists of three different ways to generate keywords: Descriptive words or phrases, YouTube video id/ url, or by Demographics.

How would you like to generate keyword ideas?

◉ Descriptive words or phrases
(e.g. green tea)

○ YouTube video id or url
(e.g. youtube.com/watch?v=JgT4aS5_Zrw)

○ Demographic ᴮᴱᵀᴬ
(e.g. male or female)

The first and default option, 'Descriptive words or phrases' lets you enter in a term and it will show related information.

Enter one keyword or phrase per line:

```
public speaking
```

☐ Don't show ideas for new keywords. I only want to see data about the keywords I entered.

(Get keyword ideas)

Type in a keyword term or phrase and click the 'Get keyword ideas' button. **Do not** select 'Don't show ideas for new keywords' unless you only want to see how many people are searching for only that one specific term.

Keywords related to term(s) entered - sorted by relevance		
public speaking	13,400	Add
public speaking tips	Not Enough Data	Add
public speaking training	Not Enough Data	Add
public speaking anxiety	Not Enough Data	Add
public speaking bloopers	Not Enough Data	Add
public speaking skills	Not Enough Data	Add
public speaking fail	Not Enough Data	Add
bad public speaking	Not Enough Data	Add
public speaking class	Not Enough Data	Add
public speaking fear	Not Enough Data	Add
self confidence	6,700	Add
debate	763,800	Add
ffa	32,500	Add
inflection	Not Enough Data	Add
farting in public	37,300	Add
mastering public speaking	Not Enough Data	Add
lonestar college	Not Enough Data	Add
inspirational speeches	45,200	Add
toast master	Not Enough Data	Add
harvard lecture	5,200	Add
goodwill hunting	4,500	Add

Depending on what keyword term or phrase you used, your results may differ from the above example. Here you will see other related terms as well as the monthly search volume and an option to add that term to your Adwords account. There may be terms that have 'Not Enough Data' in the monthly search volume as well. This means that there may be searches for these terms but not enough to formulate a number.

http://www.MarcBullard.com

That **does not** mean you should ignore these lower value keywords. This means, it may be easier for you to make videos tailored to these words. Looking at the results should provide you with ideas on tags you can use in your videos as well as ideas and topics for upcoming videos that you create. The more lower valued keywords you can place on the first page (or number 1) spot on YouTube's search results pages, the more you look like an expert in that field. This builds a relationship with the viewer, thereby increasing the odds that they'll subscribe to your channel or buy your product.

YouTube video id or url
You can search for keywords that are related to any video on YouTube. Just copy the URL of a YouTube video and paste it into the correct field. Click 'Get keyword ideas' and look at your results.

This is very handy when you want to look at your competition's tags. You can copy these tags and paste them in your videos to better optimize for SEO.

The third option is to search by demographics.

⊙ Demographic ᴮᴱᵀᴬ

(e.g. male or female)

You can search by gender, min age/max age, by country, and by interests.

Choose the demographic you wish to target.

☐ Male ☐ Female

Min Age [13 ⬍] Max Age [65+ ⬍]

Select all applicable countries; leave all boxes unchecked for the whole world.

NOTE: These countries are only used to find the demographic you want to target and are separate from the language and country selected at the top of the page for tailoring keyword and search volume results.

☐ **Americas**	☐ **Asia-Pacific**	☐ Germany	☐ Sweden
☐ United States	☐ Australia	☐ Italy	☐ Netherlands
☐ Canada	☐ Japan	☐ Israel	☐ United Kingdom
☐ Brazil	☐ **EMEA**	☐ Poland	
☐ Mexico	☐ France	☐ Spain	

Select the interests of your demographic.

All interests		Selected interests
▸ **Animals**	Add »	
▸ **Arts & Humanities**	Add »	
▸ **Automotive**	Add »	
▸ **Beauty & Personal Care**	Add »	
▸ **Business**	Add »	
▸ **Computers & Electronics**	Add »	
▸ **Entertainment**	Add »	
▸ **Food & Drink**	Add »	
▸ **Games**	Add »	
▸ **Home & Garden**	Add »	
▸ **Industries**	Add »	
▸ **Internet**	Add »	
▸ **Lifestyles**	Add »	
▸ **Local**	Add »	

(Get keyword ideas)

Searching by interest lets you choose categories or subcategories. Add these to the 'Selected interests' window and then click 'Get keyword ideas'. These keyword ideas can then be used to create targeted videos on those subjects.

A good practice would be to use numerous keyword tools when researching topics for your videos. Never rely on just one keyword tool.

Description

The next box you encounter is the Description box. The description box is a great place to enter text on what your video is about. YouTube looks at what you put in the description box, so it's good to put keywords in your description.

Now don't go typing in a list of keywords in your description box, you have to sprinkle them into your description and they have to sound natural. Take a look at a correctly formatted description below.

Description:

http://www.topinternetconsulting.com All you authors out there, start doing this right now. Book trailers are quick, easy to make videos that tell the story of your book. They are just like movie trailers except for your book. You can learn how to make these and how to market them from our Easy Video Creation training series. Also, subscribe to our channel to get the latest from us.

The first thing you see is some HTML code, more specifically, a website URL. We'll get to that in a moment. Take a look at the paragraph after the code. It gives information on the same subject as the video title above. Also, there are keywords sprinkled in such as 'book trailers', 'authors', and 'Easy Video Creation'. This is how you should have every one of your descriptions.

After the main paragraph that is relevant to that video, you can add more paragraphs that may be more general in nature. These extra paragraphs should be about your business, YouTube channel, etc. They should also have other keywords sprinkled in.

DESCRIPTION:

http://www.marcbullard.com When you upload an unlisted video, your subscribers are notified. There's an easy way to prevent this. This YouTube tutorial shows you how to disable this feature. This is using the YouTube 2014 layout.

Subscribe: http://www.youtube.com/user/videoMTC

Marc's new YouTube Marketing course at Udemy. Save $30 with this coupon: http://bit.ly/176EjBs

What's all this about? Video marketing, specifically YouTube marketing has quickly turned into one of the most powerful Internet marketing tools available. With little more than a camera and a microphone, anybody can use the power of the Internet to be seen and heard.

If you're an author, consultant, small business owner, or anybody that wants publicity online, you need to understand video marketing. Discover YouTube's secrets, implement a marketing plan, and showcase your brand like never before. It's all here. You'll find a detailed breakdown of keyword strategies, optimizing techniques for videos and channels, marketing tactics, advertising opportunities, and crucial metrics & analysis tools.

• YouTube Marketing
• Video Marketing
• Online Business
• eCommerce

Or, if time is a priority, you might be interested in Consulting Services with Marc or a Done-for-you service.
http://www.marcbullard.com
bullard.marc@gmail.com

The highlighted paragraph is specific to that video. The remaining paragraphs are more general in nature and can be used on all of your videos.

But what about that HTML code at the beginning?

The HTML code, that stuff starting with 'http://.....', is the actual website link to wherever you want your viewers to click to. This can be your blog, website, landing page, sales page, or anywhere else that you want to send your potential customers. The way it is typed out is the only way YouTube will allow a click-able link in your description box.

So why do you need to put a link to your site in the description box anyway? People watching your video may like the information you are giving them and are now interested in getting more information or purchasing your products. Putting a click-able link right there in the description box is the easiest way for them to get to your site. Sure, they could type it out, but I promise you there are people out there that are too lazy to do it. I know I'm like that sometimes. So let's make it easy for them.

Now, why did I put the URL to my site as the first thing in the description box? For a couple of reasons. Let's look at a typical YouTube page:

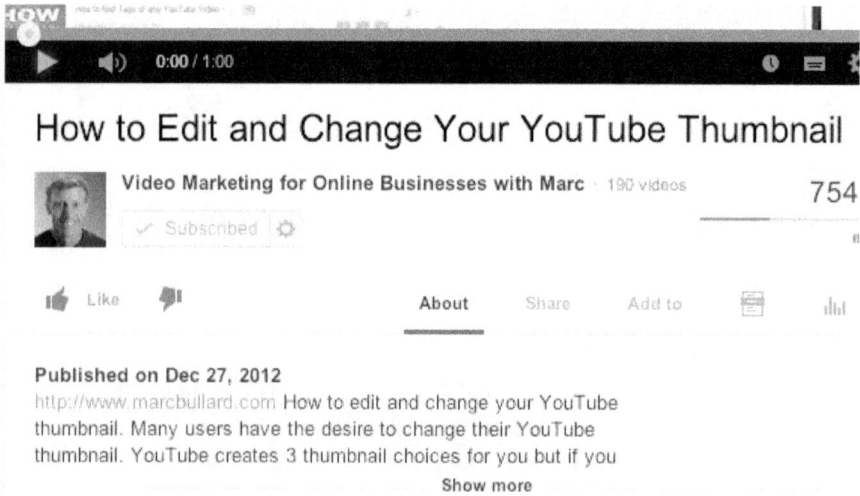

Here we see what a typical viewer gets to when he searches for and clicks on a video. In the photo above, you see the title of the video, the username

http://www.MarcBullard.com

of the uploader, and 'Subscribe' button. Under those are buttons used for liking/disliking and tabs for adding, sharing, flagging, captions, and more.

Underneath all of that you see the beginning of our description. The description is cut off but there is a button that allows you to 'Show more'. If you click on the 'Show more' button, the rest of the description can be seen; as you can see in the photo below.

Published on Dec 27, 2012

http://www.marcbullard.com How to edit and change your YouTube thumbnail. Many users have the desire to change their YouTube thumbnail. YouTube creates 3 thumbnail choices for you but if you upload enough videos, increase views, and monetize, YouTube will allow you to upload your own custom thumbnail.

This video explains the process to uploading a custom thumbnail.

CHECK OUT MY CHANNEL:
http://www.youtube.com/user/videomtc

Category   Howto & Style
License   Standard YouTube License

Show less

Once the 'Show more' button is clicked, viewers can see the rest of the description. The problem for you is that most people don't bother clicking the 'Show more' button. That means if you put your click-able link anywhere but the top of the description box, a lot of people won't see it. That's one reason why you want to put it in the beginning. The other reason to put it there is because it is located right in the line of vision to our viewer. If the viewer needs to pause, play, adjust the volume, or any number of things in the area of the video player, the link to your site is in the same general area.

Why is this link so important? Since the description box is one of three places YouTube allows you to put a click-able link to an external site, that also means it's the only place anywhere on the page that a viewer can click to your site. It's very valuable.

Tags Box

The 'Tags' box is the third most important place to optimize your video. This is another place you would put relevant keywords. It's important to fill out the 'Tags' box with keyword terms that are related to the video. You can use up to 500 characters in the tags box. A good rule of thumb is to have no more than 6-12 tags in the tags box, so pick the best, most relevant tags you can. Tags can be individual words or phrases. In order to provide its users with the best results, YouTube pays a lot of attention to tags, and that's why you should too.

If you are having trouble coming up with tags, YouTube provides you with suggestions.

You can also use the keyword tools mentioned earlier in this book. Another great tip when it comes to tags is to order your tags the same as in your title. For example, if your video title is "Business Management: Team Problem Solving Skills", your tags would be listed like the image below.

Tags

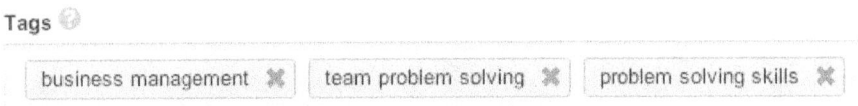

Remember, your tags should mirror your title.

Secret Word Tag Trick

If you were paying attention to the tags I used, you may have noticed a random word as the last tag. What is that? That is my secret tag.

If you've ever watched a YouTube video that wasn't on someone's channel - most people have - you will notice a bunch of related videos on the right hand side of the screen. These are suggestions – made by YouTube – to other videos you may be interested in. Looking closely at these suggestions shows that the suggested videos are from many different users. This means that after a viewer watches your video, they may click one of the others' and be on their way. This isn't too good if you're trying to get them to click to your site.

There are two ways to fix this problem. The first way is to direct traffic to your channel (more on this later). In your channel, only videos uploaded by you are available on the right hand side; but not everybody is going to find your video through your channel.

The other option is to use the secret word tag trick, it's very simple and works really well. All you have to do is create a nonsense word, like 'Jamstickerees', 'fleeblinghouse', 'wangchungington' and I could go on and on. It's fun! Anyway, create your own nonsense word and put it in with your other tags.

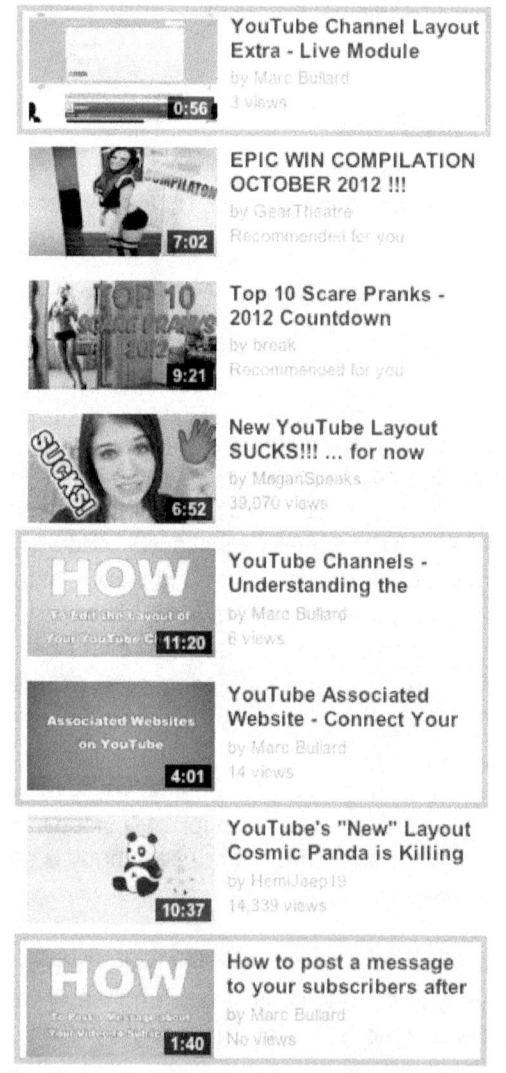

I have 4 out of 8 of the top suggested videos.

http://www.MarcBullard.com

Do this in every video that you upload and pretty soon, you will dominate the suggested videos. Why? Because YouTube sees your nonsense word and associates it with other instances of your nonsense word, which just happen to be other videos of yours.

How do you come up with your own nonsense word? Easy, start searching. Start of with any random word you can think of and type it into YouTube's search bar.

I'm going to start with the word 'blorr'.

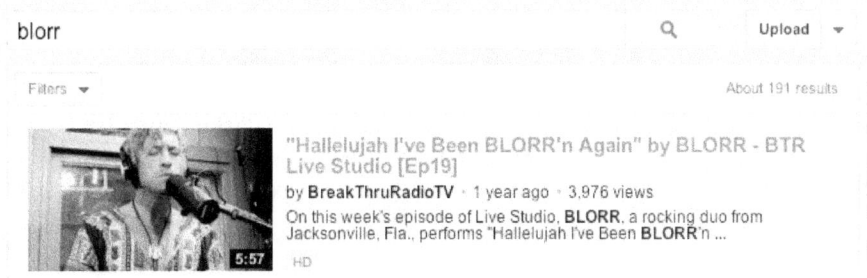

The word 'blorr' came up with about 191 results. This won't do. We need zero results. So I'm going to add to my original word.

My new word 'blorringhouse' comes up with no results. This is perfect. I can now add this word to all of my videos' tags. Now, whenever somebody watches one of my videos, YouTube will suggest videos with similar tags. Since only my videos contain the tag 'blorringhouse', more of my videos will show.

When viewers see a bunch of your videos in the suggested area, they will think you must know what you're talking about because you keep coming up in the suggested videos.

Use tags to spy on your competition
Tags are not only important in your videos; they can be a great resource to build traffic too. When you're watching other user's videos related to your field of interest - and you should - be sure to check out the tags. Other people's tags are a great place to find other terms you haven't thought of and you can find terms that would help your videos show up in other users suggested videos.

Oh no! The tags are gone. Before 2013, YouTube let everybody's tags be visible. Not anymore. That doesn't mean you can't find them. It just means you need to "get a little nerdy" in order to do it.

First, find a competitor's video. Videos with more views are usually the best to start with. Then, in your web browser, you need to view the source code of that page. Every browser has this option.

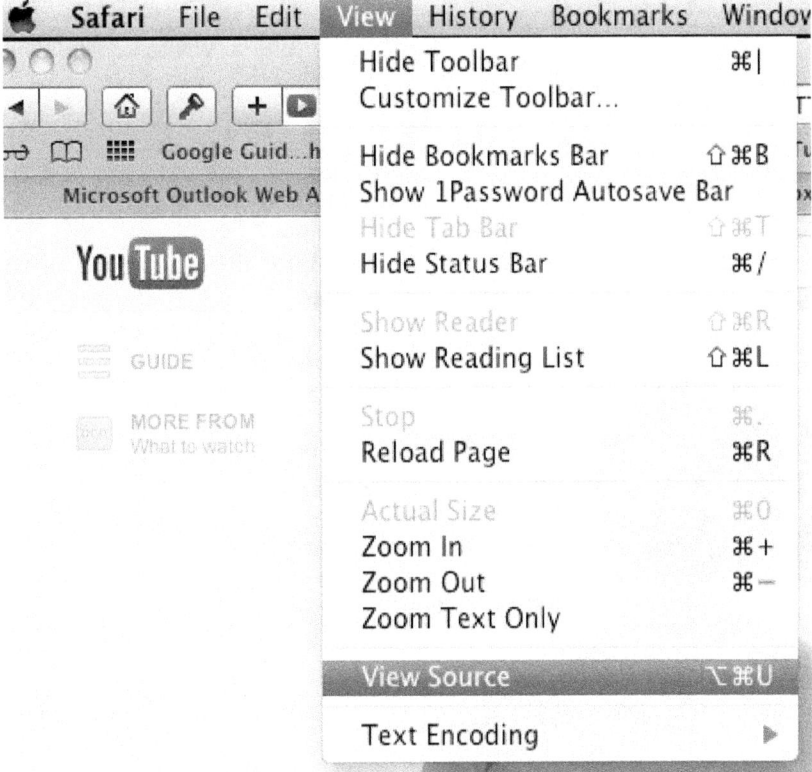

In Safari, you can view source under View>ViewSource.

Tools Window Help

Web Search	⌘K

ers React to Viral Videos Ep. #2 – YouTul

Downloads	⌘J
Add-ons	⇧⌘A
Set Up Sync...	

HostGator Contr... ▶ YouTube –

Web Developer	▶
Page Info	⌘I
Start Private Browsing	⇧⌘P
Clear Recent History...	⇧⌘⌫
S3 Organizer	

Developer Toolbar	⇧F2
Web Console	⌥⌘K
Inspect	⌥⌘I
Responsive Design View	⌥⌘M
Debugger	⌥⌘S
Scratchpad	⇧F4
Style Editor	⇧F7
Page Source	⌘U
Error Console	⇧⌘J
Get More Tools	

In Firefox, look under Tools>Web Developer>Page Source.

View History Bookmarks Window Users Help

✓ Always Show Bookmarks Bar	⇧⌘B

YouTubeMarketi

Stop	⌘.
Force Reload This Page	⇧⌘R

umns Show Navigation Gallery Toolbo

Document Elements   Quick

Enter Presentation Mode	⇧⌘F
Actual Size	⌘0
Zoom In	⌘+
Zoom Out	⌘—
Encoding	▶
Developer	▶

View Source	⌥⌘U
Developer Tools	⌥⌘I
JavaScript Console	⌥⌘J

In Chrome, look under View>Developer>View Source.

http://www.MarcBullard.com

A page will open showing a lot of code. Look through this code until you see something like this. It's usually near the top of the page.

```
<meta name="keywords" content="creator, lessons, 2012, videos, viral videos, viral, youtube,
youtube creator, youtuber, online video, most viewed videos, learn, create, content, tim
schmoy...">
```

This line of code will show you what tags were used for that video. You can now use some (or all) of these tags in your videos. This is great for getting keyword ideas for your videos. Additionally, this technique works with YouTube channels as well. Go to a competitor's channel and view the source. You can see the keywords for their channel in the code.

Privacy

Next to the title box are options to make your video Public, Unlisted, or Private. For marketing purposes, you want your videos to be Public.

Public is the best choice for most of your videos. This option lets your video be found by anybody. If you are using your videos to drive traffic, this will ensure people can find it.

Unlisted means your video is uploaded to your videos but nobody can search and find it. Since you are the one who uploaded it, you are provided all the other options to add keywords, add a description, tags, and so on.

The only people who can view an unlisted video are the people who have the URL link. Only you have the URL unless you share it. No search engine will find this type of video.

Private means the video is private and only viewable by people you designate. No search engine will find this type of video.

Scheduled means partners can schedule a Private video to go public at a later time. The video will remain private until the specified scheduled publish time. You can schedule a video publish time only if you set the video as private or scheduled on the upload landing page. The Scheduled Publishing feature allows you to precisely choose the date, time, and time zone at which you want your video to be sent to subscribers.

Below that are options to share your video with social media sites and to quickly add your video to a playlist.

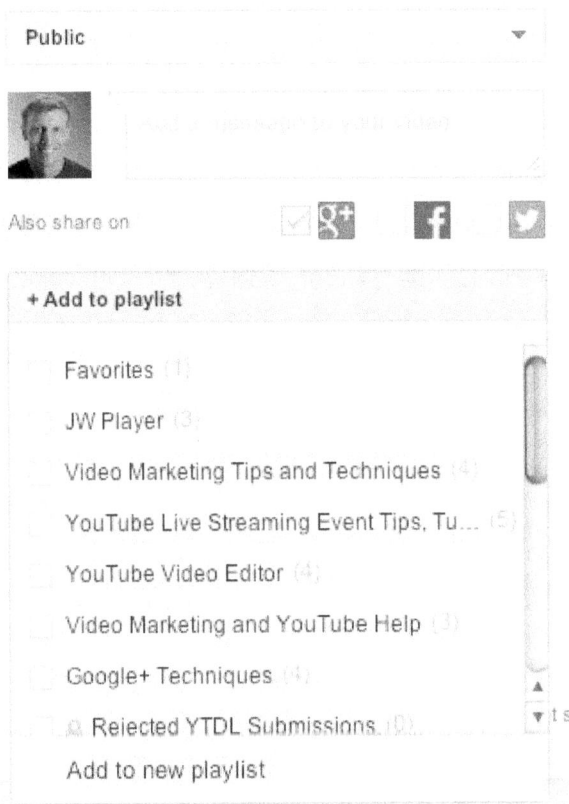

Monetization

While uploading, other tabs such as 'Monetization' and 'Advanced Settings' are available with additional features. One of those tabs is the Monetization tab.

☑ Monetize with Ads

Ad Formats

☑ Overlay in-video ads ⓘ

☑ TrueView in-stream ads ⓘ

☐ *This video contains a paid product placement* ⓘ

Display ads are shown by default. ⓘ

Syndication

● Everywhere
   make this video available on all platforms

○ Monetized platforms
   make this video available only on monetized platforms

Here, you can choose whether you want to run ads with your videos. By default the 'Monetize my video' box is unchecked.

The pros and cons to monetization will be covered later in this book. You don't have to decide to monetize the moment your video is uploading. You can turn this option off or on any time you wish.

Video Thumbnail
Another option you can change is your video thumbnail. Your video thumbnail is the still image of your video that shows up in YouTube and Google search results. The thumbnail has been known to be a huge deciding factor in people choosing your video to watch.

The video thumbnail box shows you three options (four if you have that feature enbled). YouTube will automatically pick the middle choice for you. You can pick another one if you like. If you have just uploaded your video, the thumbnail stills may not be available to you for up to 36 hours. Usually, the thumbnails will be available within a couple of minutes.

There has been a lot of conversation involved with YouTube thumbnails and how they decide what stills you can choose from. That's right, YouTube decides what stills you can use, not you. If you take a look at your own provided stills, you may be able to figure out the first thumbnail is usually taken from near the beginning of the video. The second thumbnail is usually taken from somewhere near the middle and the third taken from near the end.

Custom Thumbnail
If you monetize your videos, YouTube lets you upload a custom thumbnail. This is very beneficial to gaining viewers. Simply create a .jpg that is no

larger than 2MB and click the 'Custom thumbnail' button. Find the file you want and select it. This custom thumbnail is now available for you to use.

Custom Thumbnail Selected

Advanced Settings
The 'Advanced Settings' tab gives you even more options for your video.

Basic info   Monetization   **Advanced settings**

Comments

☑ Allow comments   Approved   ▾

☑ Users can view ratings for this video

License and rights ownership

Standard YouTube License   ▾

Syndication

Everywhere

Caption certification ⓘ

Select one   ▾

Distribution options

☑ Allow embedding ⓘ

☐ Notify subscribers ⓘ

Age restrictions

☐ Enable age restriction ⓘ

Category

Science & Technology   ▾

Video location

                                        Search

Recording date

March 12, 2014   Today

3D video

No preference   ▾

Video statistics

☑ Make video statistics on the watch page publicly visible ⓘ

Comments and responses

YouTube tries very hard to be a social site. Comments are a great way to add to the social interaction on your videos. Additionally, YouTube uses comments as a factor to determine how popular a video is. Popularity does affect rankings.

You can decide on how you want to handle comments from other users. By default, 'Allow comments' is checked and is set to 'All'. You have the option to turn off or only allow comments that you approve.

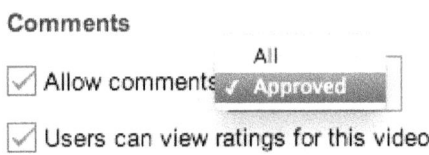

http://www.MarcBullard.com

Now, the best way to get a dialogue going which in turn can make your video very popular, is to leave the defaults, *allow comments automatically*. The problem with this option is that your comments can get filled with spam. If you keep an eye on the comments, you can moderate any that you think are spam, or you can choose to only allow comments once you approve them.

If you choose to not allow any comments, this is the worst choice when it comes to marketing and building any type of social interaction with other viewers. **It is recommended that you allow some form of commenting.**

Comment Voting
Comment voting means other viewers can rate comments with either a thumbs up or thumbs down.

Viewers who find a comment particularly helpful, funny, smart, or who just agree with that comment can vote 'up' or 'down'. The more 'up' votes a comment gets, the farther up to the top of the comment page it will go. And being closer to the top is better, meaning it will be seen more often.

Reply · 5

The blue number next to the thumbs up indicates how many 'up' votes that comment received.

You can choose to allow comments or not. It's a very good idea to allow comment voting. Again, this adds to the community feel of YouTube. It helps others participate. The more they participate, the better chance you have of them watching more videos or clicking out to your site.

Ratings
Ratings are used for viewers to vote on how much they like a particular video. The ratings are a lot like comment voting, using a thumbs up or thumbs down to vote.

This rating system can be seen located right under the username and subscribe button.

YouTube also shows the results of ratings in the green bar here:

The 2366 likes means 21 people clicked the thumbs up. The 21 dislikes means 21 people clicked the thumbs down. Allowing rating adds to the interactivity of YouTube. I recommend you leave it on. Good ratings can help you become a featured video on YouTube.

License and Rights Ownership

You have two choices: Standard YouTube License or Creative Commons. For almost all of your videos, you will want the first choice. Creative Commons means anybody can use your video, it's similar to royalty free video.

Caption certification

If your video was ever aired on television, it may be subject to FCC regulations regarding closed captioning. If this is the case, you may have to submit a caption certification.

Caption certification

✓ Select one
This content has never aired on television in the U.S.
This content has only aired on television in the U.S. without captions.
This content has not aired on U.S. television with captions since September 30, 2012.
This content does not consist of full-length video programming.
This content does not fall within a category of online programming that currently requires captions under FCC regulations.
The FCC and/or U.S. Congress has granted an exemption from captioning requirements for this content.

Distribution Options

Embedding is the act of taking a snippet of code that YouTube supplies, and putting that code on your own site or any site that will accept embed codes, which is a lot. This means if people go to another site and see your video there, they can play it. If they play your video on a site that isn't YouTube, don't fret. It still counts as a view on YouTube and all of your video information is still intact. This does not mean they can copy or edit your video in any way. It does mean that your video can be seen at a lot of different places, thereby increasing your views. This is a good thing.

Some people may not feel comfortable having their video all over the web, posted on numerous sites. If that's you, uncheck this option.

Distribution options

☑ Allow embedding

☑ Notify subscribers

Notify subscribers is also good to leave checked. This mean your subscribers will know when you upload a new video. However, there are times that you may not want your subscribers to know about a video, such as if it's an unlisted video. In that case, you should uncheck this option.

For the most part, you will want this option checked on. This is just one more way for you to spread your video all over the web, and that's a good thing.

Age Restrictions

You can check this box if you don't want young viewers to watch this video.

Age restrictions

Don't let underage users watch this
video. Learn more

☐ Enable age restriction ❓

Category

YouTube pays attention to category as one of its determining factors for
finding relevant videos. According to YouTube, after 'Music', some of the
most popular categories are 'News and Politics' or 'Comedy'.

Category

- ✓ Autos & Vehicles
- Comedy
- Education
- Entertainment
- Film & Animation
- Gaming
- Howto & Style
- Music
- News & Politics
- Nonprofits & Activism
- People & Blogs
- Pets & Animals
- Science & Technology
- Sports
- Travel & Events

If you can somehow work your content into these categories, it could help
you out. However, since these categories are the most popular, it also
means the competition could be fierce as well. If you can't fit your video into
one of these categories, don't worry about it. The other categories are still
full of videos and people looking for your information.

Video location

The 'Location' section is great for relevance and location.

Video location

Search

Clicking the 'Search' button will bring up a map that you can click on to set the location of your video. Using the map to display where the video was shot can help businesses that focus on local search. For example: a car salesman could make videos showing off the newest deals. With the added information on the map, potential customers know exactly where to go to get to the dealership. Just enter in a name or city in the 'Map Location' box and the marker will move to that destination. You can also drag the marker to your location.

Video location

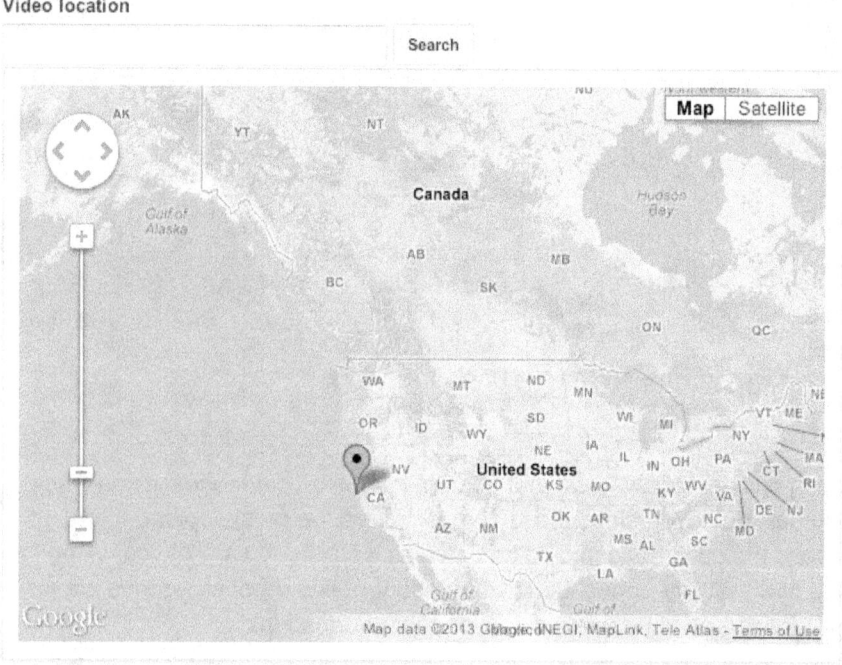

http://www.MarcBullard.com

If you are an international business, you don't have to use the map at all. Or you could create location specific videos for your services and post them up on YouTube with the appropriate location on your video's map.

Date

Dating a video can help add to its credibility as well as how current the content is. Displaying the date can be a double-edged sword. On one hand it will prove how current the content is, however, if you leave that video up for too long, the date can show how un-current your content is. If you keep up with the content and change that video every so often, the date will not cause a problem and probably help you.

Recording date

| March 12, 2014 | | | | | | | Today |

	Sun	Mon	Tue	Wed	Thu	Fri	Sat
9	23	24	25	26	27	28	1
10	2	3	4	5	6	7	8
11	9	10	11	12	13		15
12	16	17	18	19	20	21	22
13	23	24	25	26	27	28	29
14	30	31	1	2	3	4	5
Today							None

h page publicly visibl

3D

This option box is for video that utilizes 3D technology. YouTube issues a warning that changing these options will cause your video to play incorrectly. If your video is in 3D, you would want to check one of the appropriate boxes.

3D Video

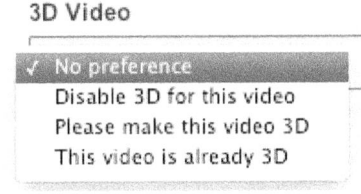

Video Statistics

Video statistics are shown on each of your videos unless you uncheck this box. Either choice won't affect search rankings.

Video statistics

☑ Make video statistics on the watch page publicly visible ❓

Video statistics show up on the watch page of your video.

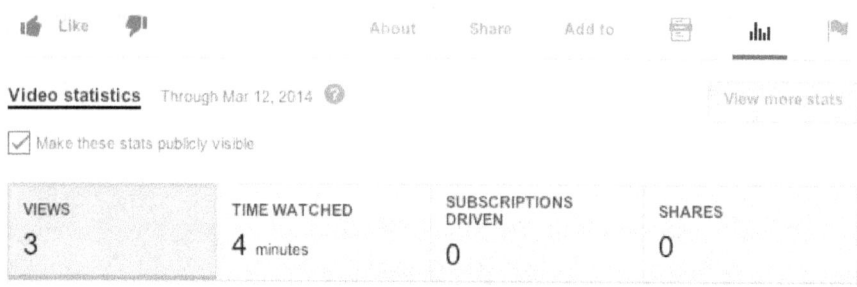

Video Statistics

Once you have entered in all the options you want for your video, there's only one more thing to do, Save changes.

Don't worry. None of these options are set in stone. You can always go back in and change any or all of these settings.

Whew. Is that it? Well, no. We still have a few more tabs to take a look at. But there won't be a lot of steps involved with the next few tabs. Or will there? (evil laugh)

http://www.MarcBullard.com

After you have saved all of the choices you selected while uploading, you still have other features that you can use to modify your video. These features are available to you after your video is uploaded and processed. There's also multiple ways to access these features.

In your Video Manager, click the down pointing arrow next to the 'Edit' button. You will see a couple of choices: 'Info and Settings', 'Enhancements', 'Audio', 'Annotations', 'Captions', 'Download MP4', 'Promote' and 'Delete'.

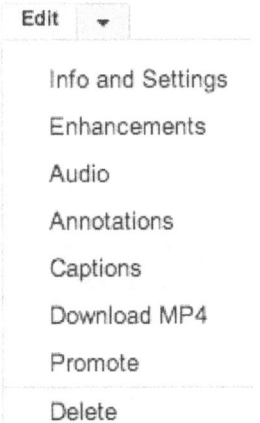

Additionally, if you click the 'Edit' button, you will be taken to that video's 'Info and Settings' page. At the top of this page are tabs to access the same links as above minus 'Download MP4' and 'Promote'.

Whatever method you choose to access these features, the next one we will look at is 'Enhancements'.

Enhancements

'Enhancements provide you with more ways to customize your video. You can add filters, fine tune the lighting, let YouTube auto-fix the lighting, stabilize shaky video, trim the beginning and end, add slow motion, and rotate the video.

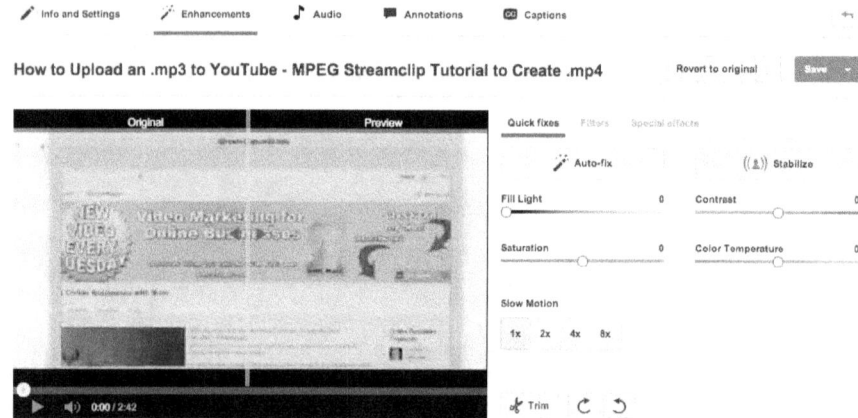

Filters
There are a lot of filters that change the look of your video. These don't help you with any aspect of marketing but can make your video stand out from others. Feel free to play around with some of the filters, you can always revert back to your original video at any point.

Lighting
You can change the lighting of your video by either choosing 'Auto-fix' or manually doing it yourself.

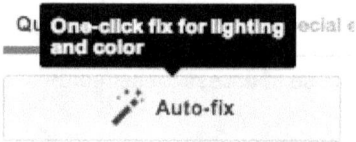

If you want to manually adjust the lighting, click the button next to 'Auto-fix' and change the settings.

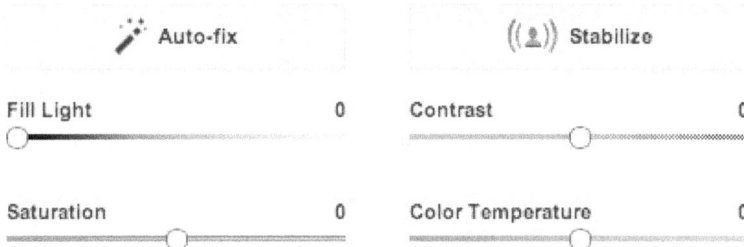

Stabilize

If you have shaky footage, YouTube can attempt to smoothen it. If you click the 'Stabilize' button, YouTube will do the rest. In my opinion, the stabilize feature doesn't work very well. The videos tend to have an underwater look to them that stands out and is distracting. Use 'Stabilize' at your own risk.

Trim

Sometimes you just need to cut off a little at the beginning or end of your video. 'Trim' lets you do this fairly easily.

If you want to trim the beginning of your video, simply click and drag the left handle to the right. If you want to trim the end of your video, simply click and drag the right handle to the left. Then click 'Done'.

Additional features

There is an additional feature on this page that lets you blur faces. If you need to obscure the identity of somebody, this is where you can do it. YouTube tries to do a good job blurring the faces. Sometimes the results aren't very desirable. Use the preview to determine if this enhancement is usable.

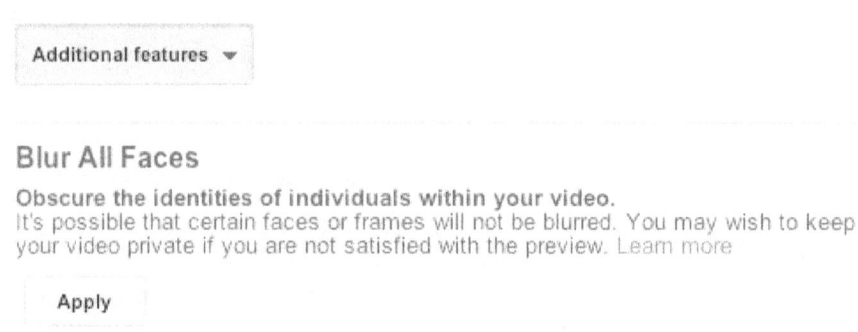

Once you have made all the enhancements you want, be sure to click 'Save'.

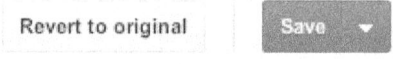

Your new enhanced video will be saved as a different video. The original video will still be available in your 'Video Manager'.

The next tab we have to deal with is the 'Audio' tab. 'Audio' sounds exactly like what it is, it's meant for swapping your video's audio track with another audio track that YouTube provides. YouTube found most of the people uploading videos contained a music track. Often, this music track violated copyright laws that YouTube had to deal with.

Usually, they let you know you're using a copy written track and that the audio will be disabled. This means your video will not have any sound whatsoever, including any narration you have. Most people don't like having a silent video so YouTube came up with the 'Audio' tab. 'Audio' is basically free, royalty free music for YouTube users to add to their videos.

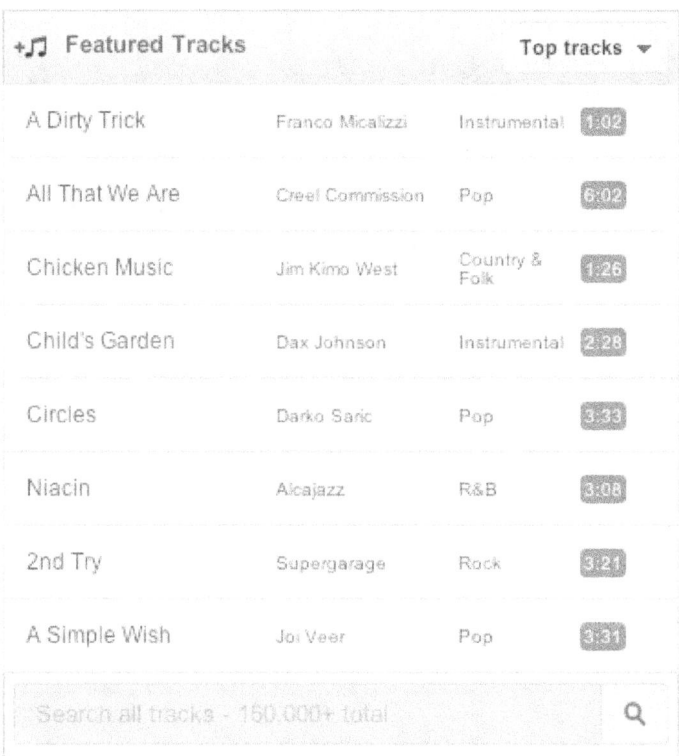

You can sort through the audio by 'Top tracks', 'Instrumental', 'Rock' and more. Clicking on a track will put it with your video and let you hear what it sounds like. You can also position the audio to fit with your video. Once you have it set how you want, click 'Done positioning' and then save your changes.

http://www.MarcBullard.com

Once your video is saved, it will not have the original audio it had when you uploaded it. Also, if your video has any narration, that will be gone too unless you choose to mix the two.

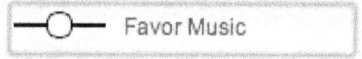

Audio is best for videos that don't have any narration, videos such as a slide show type video work best.

Annotations

Annotations is the next tab available for your video options. Annotations are YouTube's way for you to add interactive links and commentary to your videos. With annotations you can add background information about your video, create stories with multiple possibilities, link to related YouTube videos or channels, and much more.

If you look at the picture below, examples of annotations are the small link in the upper right, the voice bubble requesting 6 cards, and the text link at the bottom of the screen. YouTube lets you create as many of these as you want. It's up to you to find creative ways to use them.

Interactive card trick

http://www.MarcBullard.com

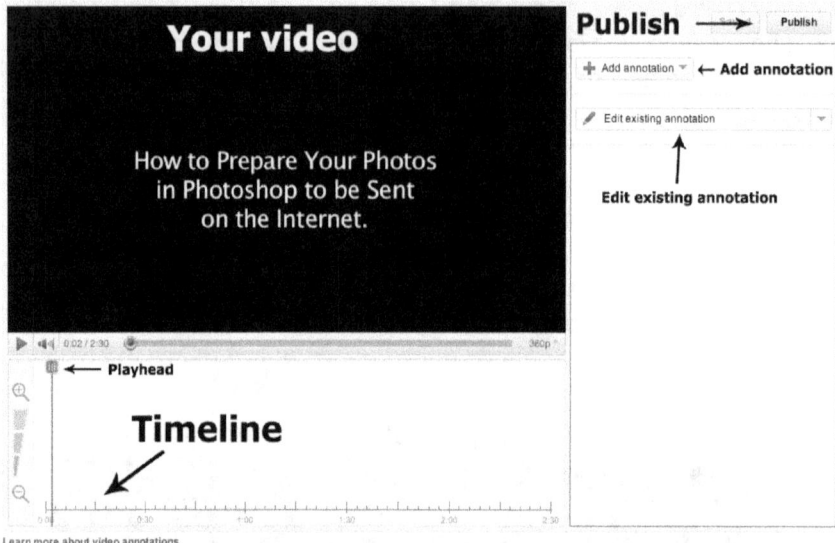

Learn more about video annotations

The annotations page contains your video, a timeline, Add annotation button, Edit existing annotation drop down, and publish button.

Adding annotations is pretty straightforward. Drag the play head to the exact location in your video that you'd want to put an annotation. Then click the Add annotation button.

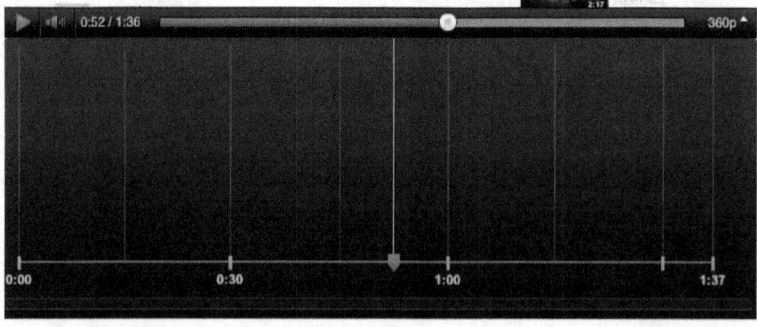

http://www.MarcBullard.com

The play head is in the location I want my annotation.

Choose what type of annotation you want to use. The types of annotations do different things such as:

Speech bubble - for creating pop-up speech bubbles with text.
Note - for creating pop-up boxes containing text.
Title - for creating a text overlay to title your video.
Spotlight - for highlighting areas in a video; when the user moves the mouse over these areas the text you enter will appear.
Label: for creating a label to call out and name a specific part of your video.

Once you have selected which type of annotation you want to insert, the following steps will allow you to fully customize the annotation:

1. You can move the annotation that you have created around the video player, customizing its location, or even changing its size and dimensions. To control the position of the annotation with maximum precision, you may select it and adjust it one pixel at a time with your arrow keys, or ten pixels at a time if you hold down 'shift' while pushing the arrow keys.
2. In the Annotations properties panel on the right, you can change the following properties of the text and annotation:

The first option changes font size. The second option changes font color, the third option is fill color. Fill color will change the background color of the box that your text is in.

Below the font and box options you should see options for setting when you want to start seeing the annotation as well as an option to specify when you want to stop seeing the annotation.

Additionally, you can do the same thing by sliding the red highlighted section in your timeline.

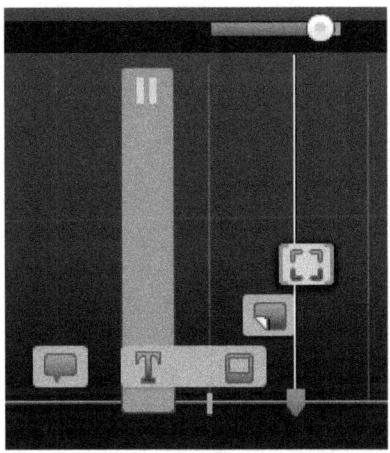

If you grab either one of the darker end sections, you can drag to specific times in your timeline.

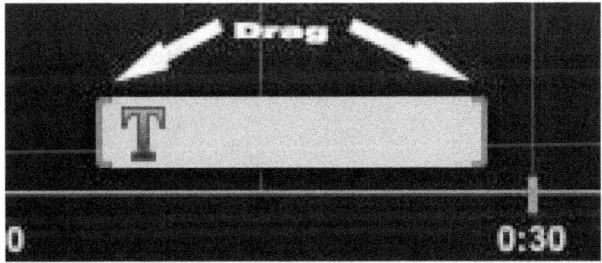

Your video is also available on the same page in order to check your annotation.

Below the time options is a check box for a link. If you check that box, you then get options to put a link in your annotation.

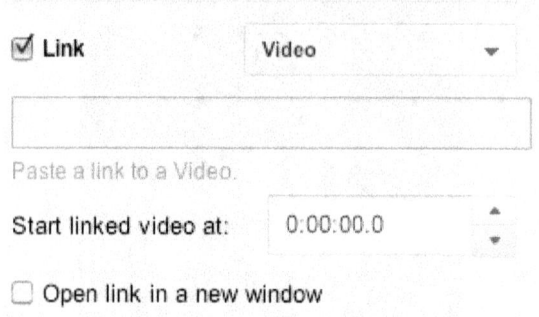

The drop down box provides different types of link options.

YouTube instructs you on what to do depending on what type of link you choose.

Video Links - Paste a link to a Video. You can copy and paste a link to any video in YouTube.

Playlist - Paste a link to a YouTube play list.

Channel - Paste a link to a YouTube channel.

Google+ Profile/Page – Paste a link to your Google+ profile or page.

Subscribe - Enter a YouTube user name to subscribe to. *Usually, this would be your YouTube user name.

Fundraising Project – You can past a link to an external fundraising site such as Kickstarter, Rockethub, Causes, Indiegogo, and more.

Associated Website – If you are a verified partner you can link to an associated website. This is an external link to your website. You need to have this site verified before you can put this link in your annotations.

Merch – You can paste a link to certain merchandising retailers such as StubHub, Rally.org, Mashon, and more. This can link to your merchandise.

Annotations can backfire on you. A lot of viewers think they are annoying and they simply turn annotations off with a simple click of a button. So don't go spending enormous amounts of time with annotations, but it doesn't hurt to try a few out.

Annotations are just another way to connect all of your videos with others. And that should be the ultimate goal: Create a networked web between all of your videos, channels, sites, etc.

*Bonus Tip: If you are one of those viewers who doesn't like annotations popping up, you can turn them off either by clicking the gear:

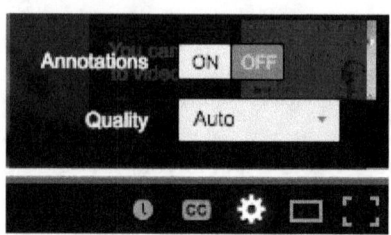

or, if you want to stop clicking the gear every single time you watch another video, go to your user name at the top right section of YouTube and click the drop down box. Then click 'YouTub Settings'.

YouTube

My channel
Video Manager
Subscriptions
YouTube settings

Sharing

Privacy

Email

Playback

CHANNEL SETTINGS

Features

Monetization

Defaults

InVideo Programming

Associated Website

Video playback quality

● Always choose the best quality for

☐ Always play HD on fullscreen (v

○ I have a slow connection. Never pl

Annotations

☑ Show annotations on videos

Captions

☑ Always show captions

☐ Show automatic captions by speec

On the 'Playback' page uncheck 'Show Annotations on videos'
Make sure to Save your changes and that's it, no more annotations.

Captions

The tab after *Annotations* is *Captions.* YouTube likes to make watching video online as easy as possible for everybody. In order to help hearing impaired viewers, YouTube offers *Captions.* You have two choices on how you can submit a caption for your video. You can either upload a caption file by clicking the upload button or you can use automatic captions.

Some people find it easier to submit a transcription. In order to do that, click the 'Upload caption file or transcript' button. Once you do, you'll be asked to choose your transcript file and then taken to this page:

optimizeplaylist.mp4

○ Caption file (includes time codes)
● Transcript file

Language   Track name

| English ▼ | Optional |

| Upload | Cancel |

There are two different types of file you can upload. The first one is a *caption file*. This file contains the text and the exact times in the video that the text was said. A caption file is usually made by special captioning companies or possibly the person who created the video. An uploaded caption file needs to be a certain type of file. Here's the file types YouTube allows:

.srt - SubRip - only the basic version is supported.
.sbv - SubViewer
.scc - Scenarist Closed Caption. For any premium content that has broadcast-quality captions (movies, TV shows, etc) we highly recommend this format.

Most people will not have a caption file, which is fine, because the next option, *Transcript File* is perfect for that.

A *transcript file* is going to be a text file of what was said in your video. You can create one of these by either watching the video and writing down everything that was said, or if you have a script, you can use that.

Upload caption file or transcript

Active tracks

English   automatic captions

YouTube tries to do a good job of creating a transcription of your video all by itself. If you click 'automatic captions' under the Available Caption Tracks, you can view how good of a job YouTube does trying to figure out what is being said.

Each video is different, but the one I tried had a lot of nonsensical words in the transcription. You would need to correct YouTube's transcription before it's usable.

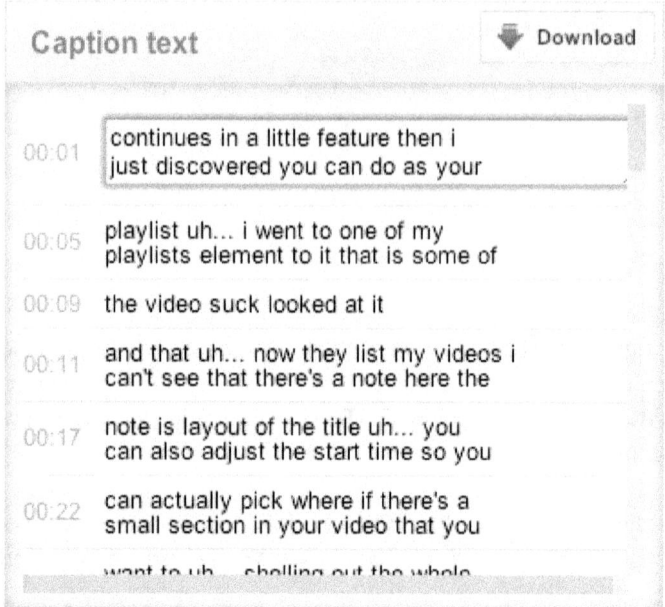

Edit YouTube's transcript in the Caption text box.

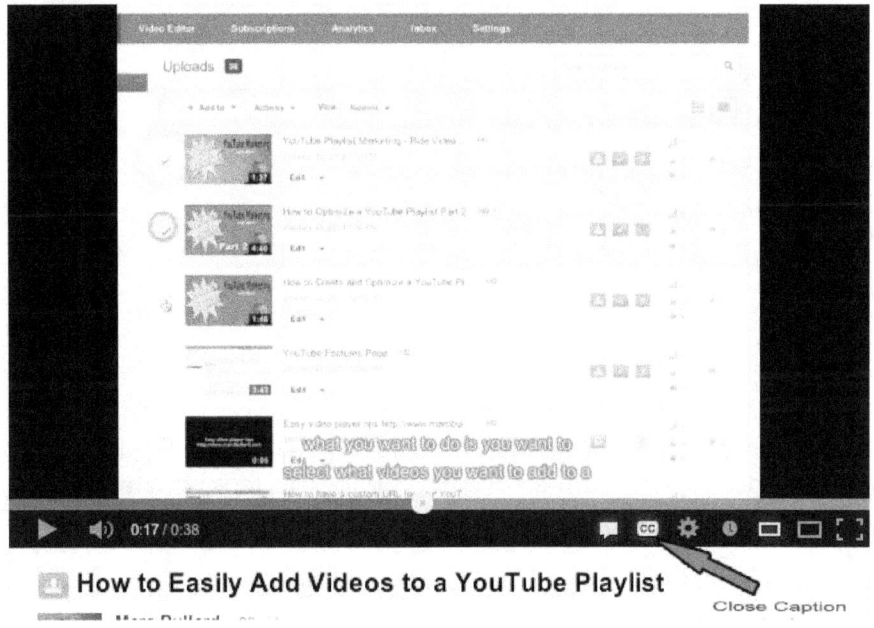

How to Easily Add Videos to a YouTube Playlist

Close Caption

When you view your video again, click the 'Closed Caption' button (CC) next to your annotations button. If you click the 'CC' button, subtitles of your text file will be visible. Another cool feature that your video now has is the 'Interactive Transcript' button.

If you click the 'Interactive Transcript' button, your transcript will show up.

http://www.MarcBullard.com

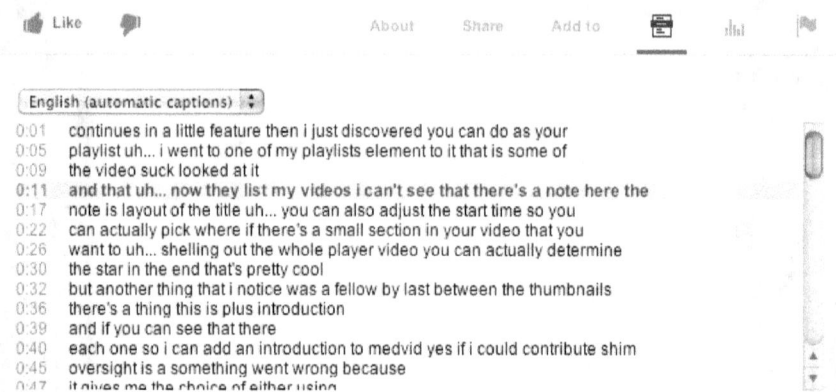

This transcript pops up in the description box and will scroll through your text as your video plays. Pretty neat, huh? And it's helpful for search results as well.

YouTube (and Google) is doing everything it can to make videos be searchable. Unfortunately, the technology is not quite there yet, but it will be. In the meantime, one of the best ways to make your video have extra search engine juice is to add a transcript. Transcripts are text, and search engines like text.

With an added transcript, you make it a lot easier for search engines to find you. If you click around YouTube and watch some of your competitor's videos, you may see a lot of them are not using the transcript option. Either they don't know about it, or are lazy and don't want to bother. Whatever the reason, it's good news to you. With a transcript, your videos may start to show up higher than theirs, and that's always good.

Video Manager Extras

When you're on the Video Manager, each video has an 'Edit' button and a downward pointing arrow. This arrow gives you access to pages such as

'Info and Settings', 'Enhancements', and more. All of these have been previously covered except the last two: 'Download MP4' and 'Promote'.

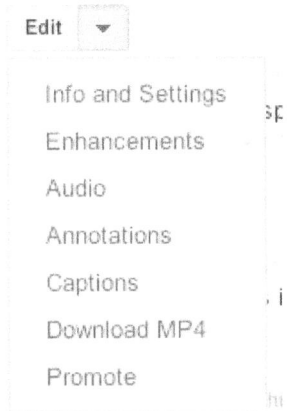

'Download MP4' will let you download an MP4 version of that video. Usually, an MP4 file is recommended so you might have this already saved on your computer. But, if you lost the original file or in a situation that you aren't at your computer but still need the file, you can download it this way.

'Promote' is used to start a video ad campaign. You will be taken to a page that asks if you want to start a campaign.

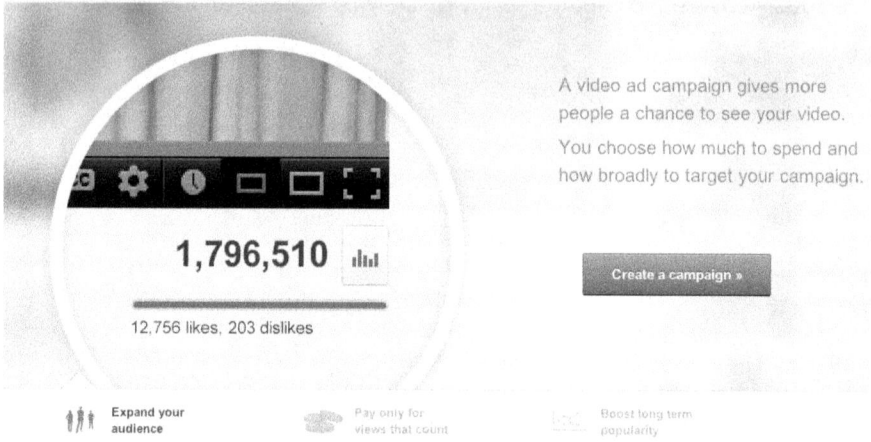

Promoting your video is a paid service you can use with YouTube. You can create a video ad that will play before another video starts. You only pay if the viewer watches for 30 seconds or to the end of the ad, whichever comes first. There are many more intricacies to promoting your video. Make sure you are well prepared to handle budgets and analytics to use it to its full potential.

Advanced Features and Bulk Editing
YouTube's Video Manager let's you edit information as well as change the settings to multiple videos at once.

If you place a check next to the videos you want to edit and click the 'Actions' drop down, you will find options to change monetization, privacy, license, and advanced features. Any changes you make will effect all checked videos.

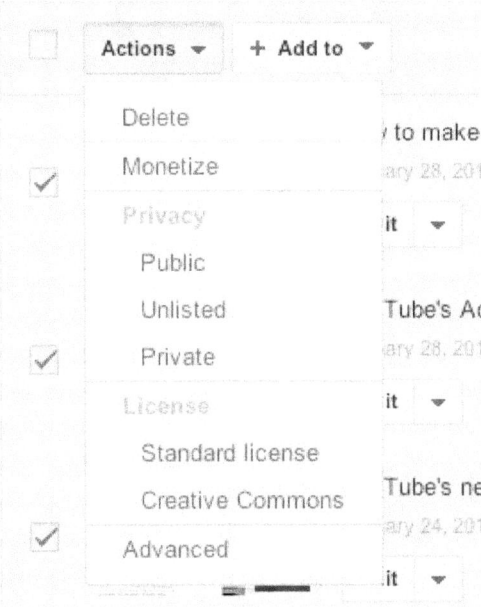

Selecting the 'Advanced' option provides you with more choices.

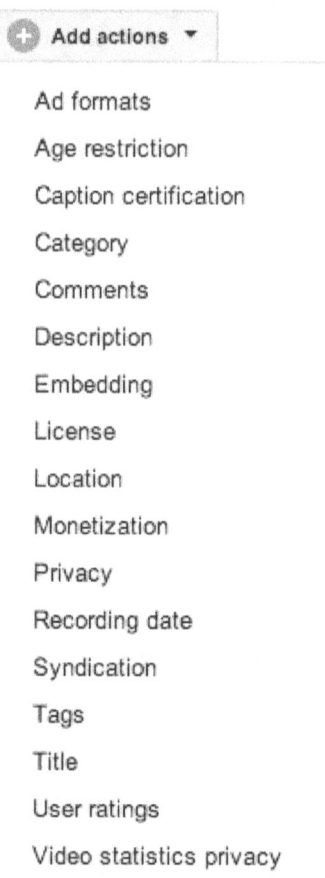

Let's say you wanted to change the 'Category' of multiple videos. Once they were checked and you clicked through 'Actions' to 'Advanced', you would select 'Category'.

The 'Category' dropdown allows you to choose what category you want. Once saved, this will change the category of every selected video. If you change your mind, you can always click the minus sign next to the word 'Category'. This will remove your latest category choice. As long as you don't hit save, removing the category won't effect your individual video's category that you previously had.

You can also add more than one action by clicking the 'Add actions' drop down. Let's say I wanted to change the category and tags to my selected videos. By clicking on 'Add actions', I can add tags to my list of actions.

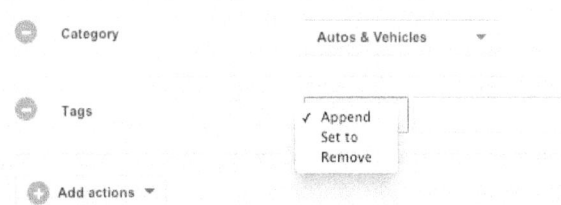

The 'Tags' action gives you the ability to add tags that will be applied to all of your selected videos. Additionally, you can add these tags to the tags you originally have (Append), set the tags to what you enter in the tags box (Set to), or remove specific tags from your selected videos (Remove).

Once you click 'Submit' ('Save' for singular actions), your selected videos will have the updated changes. This is a great way to make bulk changes to videos. Once you start accumulating more videos, you'll see why this feature is so handy.

http://www.MarcBullard.com

Views

Now that you know how to upload a video and optimize it for YouTube, it's time to start getting views. Getting views is one of the most important things you need in order to market online. Imagine the number of views as dollar bills, of course you want a high number that continues to rise. The more views, the more chances of getting a customer.

YouTube loves views. YouTube likes to showcase the 'Most Viewed' videos of the day, week, month, year, and all time. Views can also help your video achieve 'Most Popular' as well as other accolades, not to mention high view count equates to more credible the business to most viewers.

There are a lot of techniques to increase your YouTube views. You don't have to do all of them, but the more you do, the better the result. So let's get started.

Sharing and Social Networking

Sharing your video includes posting it on your social media outlets, on multiple video sharing sites, to your email list, friends, family, etc.

Social Media Sites
Social media sites such as Facebook, Myspace, hi5, Orkut, and more are great places to show your video. These sites work best when you form relationships with other users. Once you have friends on these sites, you can suggest your video to all of them. This suggestion will also be seen by all of their friends as well. They in turn, will watch it and pass it on to their friends hopefully. This cycle can repeat over and over again, thereby increasing your views.

Sharing a video on Facebook

http://www.MarcBullard.com

Since Facebook is the largest social media site to date, we'll focus on how to market with your video on there. Most of the other popular social media sites will allow you to link to video in a similar fashion. Here's how to share a video on Facebook:

Before you log in to Facebook, you need to get a small piece of code from your video that's now on YouTube. Go to YouTube and find the video you want to share. There are a lot of different ways to find your video. One of the easiest is to log in to YouTube, go to 'Video manager' and find your video. Click on your video's title or thumbnail to play the video. In order to get the code from this page you need to click the 'Share' button.

When you click the 'Share' button, the box drops down and you see this:

The first thing you see is a box with some highlighted text. This is the video's URL. You need to copy the highlighted URL by either using the keyboard shortcut control/command + C or by right clicking and selecting 'Copy'*.

*On a side note, the code that you copied can also be put in emails, .pdf or Word documents, blog comments, forum posts, etc. and it will still be a clickable link. Once clicked on, it will take people to your video on YouTube.

Now that you have the code copied, it's time to log in to Facebook. Logging in requires a free account that you must set up. Once that is set up or if you already have a Facebook account, log in. Once logged in, paste the code onto your wall, right in the status box.

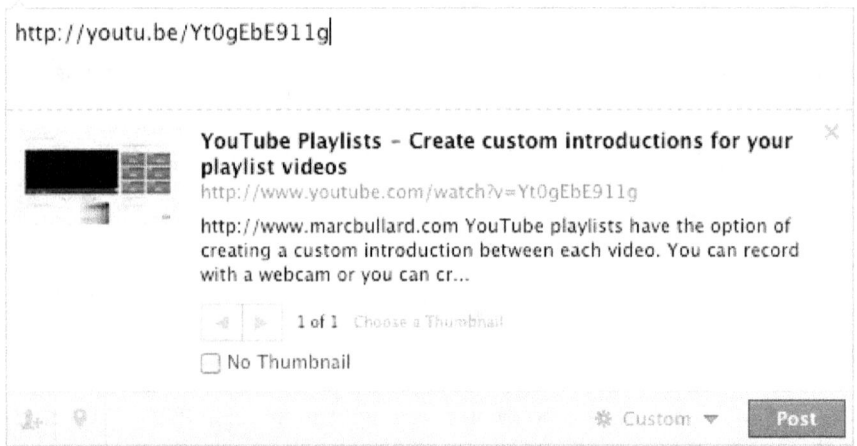

Click in the status box and paste your code in there either by using the keyboard shortcut control/command + V or by right clicking and selecting 'Paste'.

When you paste the code into your status box, Facebook recognizes what the video is. All you have to do is hit the 'Post' button and that's it. All of your friends will now see that you posted a video. Every time somebody clicks 'play' in *Facebook* to watch your video, a view gets added to that video in *YouTube*. Your friends can watch it on Facebook, they never leave the site to go watch your video. This is extremely powerful.

http://www.MarcBullard.com

Not only do you make it easy for the lazy people to watch a video by not forcing them to go to another site, but you now have the power of Facebook pushing your views.

Here is a great way to increase your views on Facebook:

Post your video to your wall. After you've posted on it, click the 'Like' link on that post and also leave a comment. The comment should be something to get other people to respond - "Tell me what you think about this subject" - or to simply pass it on - "Send this to everybody you love".

You want to get conversations going, this forms relationships and builds trust. Using the comment to get others to comment or spread your video is a great idea. Your friends have their own friends who you may not know. Those friends also have friends and so on and so on. If your video gets spread and keeps spreading, you will be gaining popularity and views.

When you are in Facebook, you may notice there is a link for 'Video'. So why didn't we use that?

We didn't use the 'Video' link because that is used to upload a video directly to your Facebook account. Our goal was to increase YouTube views, so we had to use the YouTube link. The next thing I would do, however, is I would upload the same video to Facebook by clicking on this link. This will give you the option to record a video using your web cam or uploading from your computer.

I would choose to upload from my computer and then I would select the video file from my hard drive, the same video file that I uploaded to

YouTube, and then upload that to Facebook. Now, your video will always be available to be seen on your Facebook page as well.*

*Make sure you post your YouTube link on your wall BEFORE you ever upload the same video file directly to Facebook. The YouTube link should be the first time anybody has seen your video. More people will be inclined to see it, thereby increasing views.

Hey wait, didn't I see the Facebook icon underneath the share code? Yes, you did. Good job, eagle eyes.

Yes, there is a Facebook button. If you click it, you will be asked to log in to Facebook. After you've logged in, it will share your link on your wall. So basically, it does the same thing. And faster. You got me, I showed you the long way. Why? Why would I waste your valuable time showing you the long way and not this super easy way?

Now that you know where to get your little piece of code, you can spread it out everywhere. Also, just because there's a link to share your video on Facebook, there are a lot of other great places to post your video that don't have a special button down there. For those instances, you'll need to know how to do it my way. So there. :)

Microblog sites
Microblog sites like Twitter, Jaiku, Tumblr, etc. are making it easier to post videos. Twitter has made it easy to show a video while still in the Twitter interface. Before this change, it was hard to get people to leave Twitter in

http://www.MarcBullard.com

order to watch a video from YouTube. Twitter's integration with embed codes makes it a great resource to get your video seen. If you don't have a Twitter account, sign up for one. It's free and a great tool to market your business.

Since Twitter is **THE** man when it comes to ruling the microblogospere, I'll show you how to post a video on there. Posting a video on Twitter is a lot like how you would do it on Facebook. And yes, there's even a simple easy button to post your video for you. Here's how you would do that.

Find your video that you want to share. Click the 'Share' button. Underneath the code, you'll see the button to share on Twitter (it looks like a bird). Click that button. It will ask you to log into your Twitter account. Once you are logged in, Twitter will come up with the link for you to share.

If everything looks good on your end, click 'Tweet'. Your post and video are now on Twitter.

Just so you know, the slower albeit just as functional method of copying your YouTube link and pasting it into your Twitter post will get you the same results.

Social Bookmarking Sites

Social Bookmarking Sites like Reddit, Stumbleupon, and more are great tools to get views of your video. These sites have a lot of similarities with Social Media sites such as having users, a commenting option, profiles, and more.

The difference between media and bookmarking sites is that bookmarking sites are where users submit links to other sites that users may be interested in. Social bookmarking sites break down the suggestions by categories such as keywords, audio files, documents, and video. These sites make it easy to submit your video to a large audience.

Reddit is one of the most popular social bookmarking sites so we'll focus on that one for this example. It's advisable to have accounts on multiple social bookmarking sites. They're all free and can be done quickly.

Once you log into Reddit, click the 'Submit Link' button located at the top of the page.

Submit a link

After you click on the button, a small window will open, asking for the link.

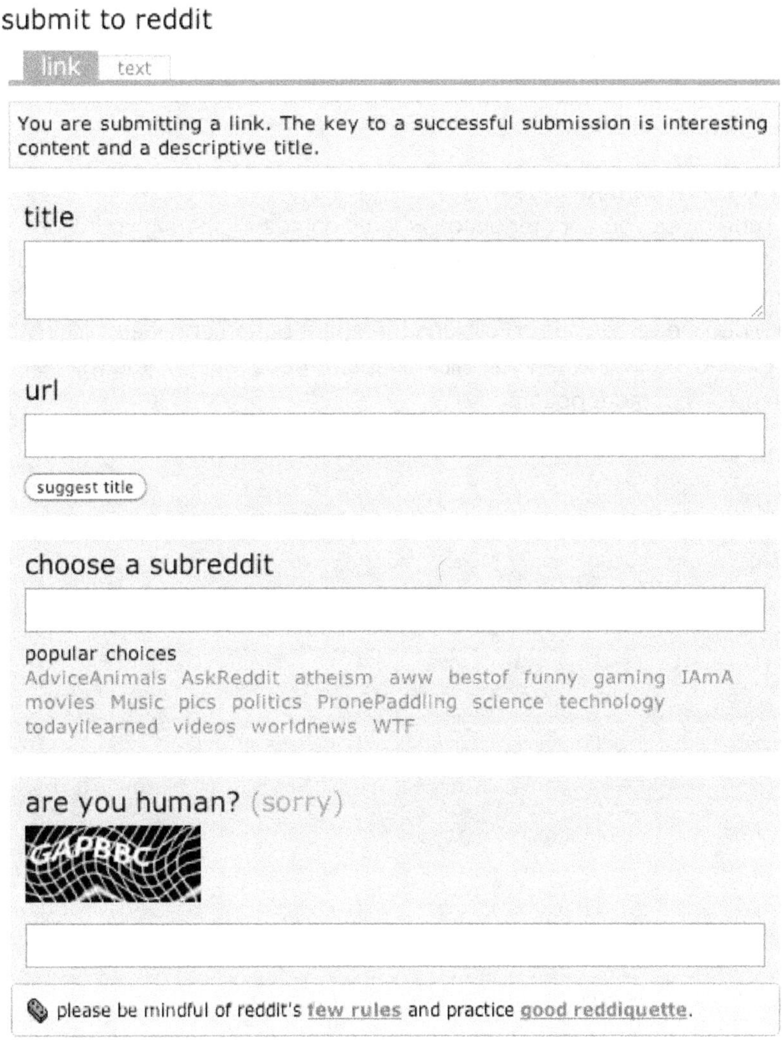

submit to reddit

link   text

> You are submitting a link. The key to a successful submission is interesting content and a descriptive title.

title

url

(suggest title)

choose a subreddit

popular choices
AdviceAnimals AskReddit atheism aww bestof funny gaming IAmA movies Music pics politics PronePaddling science technology todayilearned videos worldnews WTF

are you human? (sorry)

GAPBBC

🔖 please be mindful of reddit's few rules and practice good reddiquette.

Enter in the correct information. Try to make your title full of relevant keywords. Also, be sure to pick an appropriate subreddit. These are categories that you can use to better place your submission. And that's it.

http://www.MarcBullard.com

Just so you know, the social networking site Stumbleupon.com loves video. It's not as widely popular as Reddit but I've noticed in my analytics that Stumbleupon constantly provides results. Be sure to check it out.

Sharing with embed codes

YouTube gives you another option when it comes to sharing your video; embed codes. An embed code is a little piece of code that you can put into your website, blogs, Facebook apps, and a whole lot more. You can access your video's embed code by clicking the share button and then clicking on the 'Embed' button. When you click on the 'Embed' button, you will be presented with more options.

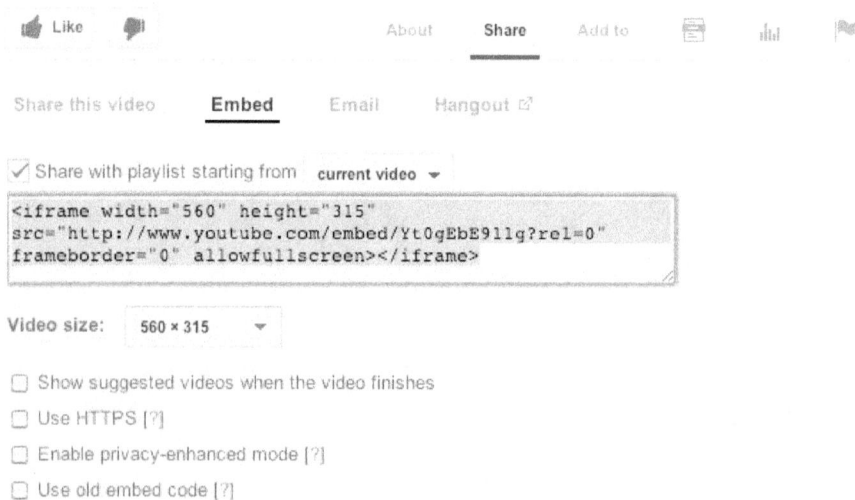

The highlighted code (in green) is your actual embed code. If you wanted your video to play in a YouTube player on some other website, all you would have to do is copy this code and then enter it into any place that accepts the code. For example, if I was going to put this video on our Wordpress blog as a post, the first thing I would do is copy the code. Then I would log into my

http://www.MarcBullard.com

Wordpress site. Once in Wordpress, I would create a new post. In the editor that opens, I click on the HTML tab. This tab accepts code.

HTML Tab

Paste the embed code in this tab.

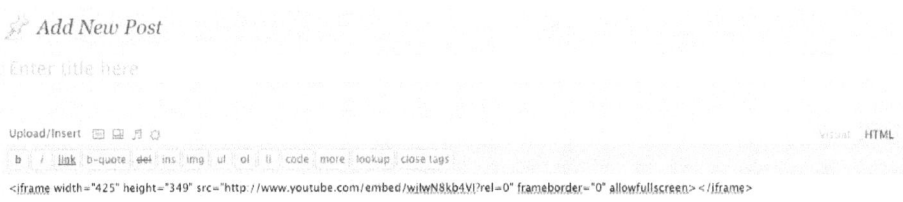

Click the 'Update' button and take a look at the site.

http://www.MarcBullard.com

The YouTube video shows up in my blog.

YouTube gives you some options to customize your video within the embed code.

http://www.MarcBullard.com

Share this video   **Embed**   Email

```
<iframe width="853" height="480"
src="//www.youtube.com/embed/filRVKqxAAA?rel=0"
frameborder="0" allowfullscreen></iframe>
```

Video size: 853 × 480   ▾

☐ Show suggested videos when the video finishes

☐ Enable privacy-enhanced mode [?]

☐ Use old embed code [?]

Show suggested videos when the video finishes - This means at the end of your video, other videos will be suggested to the viewer. A lot of people get scared that once their video is finished, the viewer may become interested in the suggested videos and click to watch one of those. This might cause them to leave your site and go to YouTube, never to return again. There goes your sale. If you uncheck this box, you don't have to worry about that ever again.

Enable privacy-enhanced mode - YouTube has it set up so they generate cookies in order to store data about the user watching a video. In order to give more options over cookies, YouTube provided this option. If this is checked, it restricts YouTube's ability to set cookies. YouTube may still set cookies on the user's computer once the visitor clicks on the video player, but it won't store personally-identifiable cookie information for videos that are embedded using the privacy enhanced mode.

Use old embed code - There are two styles of embed codes. The new version supports Flash and HTML5 video and begins with "<iframe...."

http://www.MarcBullard.com

```
<iframe width="425" height="349" src="http://www.youtube.com/embed/wjIwN8kb4VI?rel=0"
frameborder="0" allowfullscreen></iframe>
```

The old code only supports Flash playback and begins with "<object....".

```
<object width="425" height="349"><param name="movie"
value="http://www.youtube.com/v/wjIwN8kb4VI?version=3&amp;hl=en_US&amp;rel=0"></param
><param name="allowFullScreen" value="true"></param><param name="allowscriptaccess"
value="always"></param><embed
src="http://www.youtube.com/v/wjIwN8kb4VI?version=3&amp;hl=en_US&amp;rel=0"
type="application/x-shockwave-flash" width="425" height="349" allowscriptaccess="always"
allowfullscreen="true"></embed></object>
```

Some sites still haven't caught up to the times and won't allow the newer code. If that's the case, use the older code. Other than that, always use the newer code.

Dimensions - You can choose how big or small you want the video to be by picking one of the predetermined sizes or by manually typing in the dimensions in the 'Custom' boxes.

Video size: 1280 × 720   ▼

Comments
Comments can be powerful to your videos and on other user's videos. Comments on your video will help get more views, and more love from YouTube. Comments are a big deal to YouTube because they form the backbone to socializing on YouTube. YouTube is always on the lookout for the most commented videos; if you can build comments and start a conversation, it will help you move up to the top of YouTube's search results and be featured on many of YouTube's highlight pages, such as 'Most Discussed'.

So how do you get comments? One great way is by commenting yourself. Your goal is to leave a comment that will either start a conversation, get people to click your YouTube channel, or provide great additional information. Find other videos that are related to your subject or keywords and leave comments that are engaging or that contribute to the information in the video. Any time you leave a comment, your channel name is shown. People can click on your name and go to your channel.

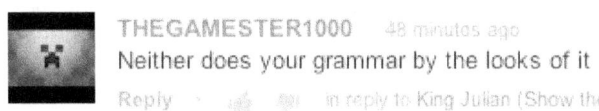

THEGAMESTER1000   48 minutes ago
Neither does your grammar by the looks of it
Reply   ·   in reply to King Julian (Show the

Can I put a click-able link in *comments*? Unfortunately no, you cannot put a click-able link in the comments section, that's why your channel name is so important. Comments are a great way to get a discussion started. Discussions lead to people coming back, which results in more views.

Now, YouTube wants your Google+ account associated with commenting. This means, along with the username, there is also an avatar to better personalize the user.

Comments get voted on and responded to
That's right, the YouTube community is allowed to vote on comments. Comment voting means other viewers can rate comments with either a thumbs up or thumbs down.

Viewers who find a comment particularly helpful, funny, smart, or which just agrees with what they were going to say can vote 'up' or 'down' on that comment. The more 'up' votes a comment gets, the better the chance it will reach the top of the comment page. And being closer up on the top is better, because it means it will be seen more often.

UnlistedRX   3 months ago
Wow!! Thank you!
Reply ·

You can respond to others' comments as well. This is a great way to get people coming back to your videos as well as engaging with your potential customers.

ZonaStudio laurent   3 months ago
I have Intel i7 Nvidia GTS 450 mother board asus p8h67. i instal lion i have 10.7.5 mac pro im noob i want to enable hight quality resolution and its my intel working at 100% ? if you can explain me what to do please.
Reply ·

Alberto Egea   3 months ago
Well, Graphics enabler-YES
Reply ·   in reply to ZonaStudio laurent

A response to a comment will appear below the original comment with an indented response. Be sure to leave text comments on your own videos as well as on other user's videos. The more comments you make, the more often your username appears. Comments that are helpful or expand on the original video usually receive higher praise from the community.

http://www.MarcBullard.com

YouTube Channels

YouTube channels are your own TV station on the Internet. Channels are extremely important and a lot of people aren't taking advantage of using them.

Your YouTube channel is a place for others to connect with you. It showcases the videos you have uploaded as well as provides information about you, your websites, and your activity on YouTube. Your channel also gives others the opportunity to contact you, leave comments, and watch other videos you have uploaded. A nice bonus to your channel is the fact that only your videos will be visible. This means there is less of a chance for somebody to click on others' videos, and in turn leaving your channel. Additionally, your channel is another place to optimize with keywords. You can provide a link to your website, connect with other channels, brand you or your company, and a lot more.

In order to access the back end of your channel, click your user name. A drop down will show you links. Click the "My Channel" link.

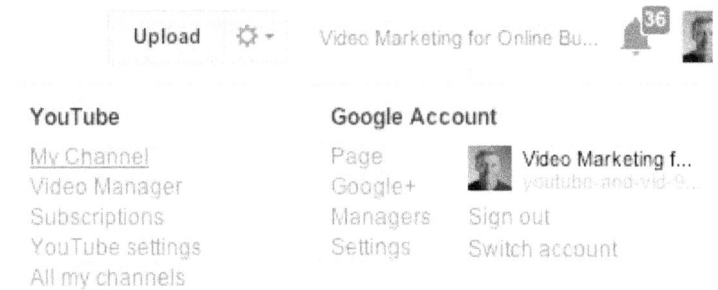

This will take you to your channel.

Your channel has the option to have different layouts as well as a custom banner graphic. You can also show a 'Channel Trailer' video, which is showcased in the middle of the channel.

Your channel has main tabs for visitors, those are: 'Home', 'Videos', 'Playlists', 'Channels', 'Discussion', 'About' and a search feature.

Video Marketing for Online Businesses with Marc

Home   Videos   Playlists   Channels   Discussion   About   🔍

The 'Home' tab is set as the default tab. This shows visitors your channel trailer and customizable sections such as Recent Uploads, Playlists, and more. The information that is shown below the channel trailer is dependant upon how you choose to lay it out.

Recent uploads

 YouTube Categories Have Moved
3 days ago · 8 views
http://www.marcbullard.com YouTube categories are now missing from the Info and Settings page as well as the ...

 Top 10 Youtube Updates for 2014
4 days ago · 42 views
YouTube has changed so much in the last year. It's time now to look at all of the new features YouTube has to off...

 How to Upload an .mp3 to YouTube - MPEG Streamclip Tutorial to Create .mp4
5 days ago · 4 views
Subscribe: http://www.youtube.com/user/videoMTC ...

 How to Add a Still Image to JW Player While Using Amazon S3
5 days ago · 4 views
Subscribe: http://www.youtube.com/user/videoMTC ...

 How To Keep Subscribers From Being Notified of Unlisted Video Uploads - 2014
1 week ago · 20 views
http://www.marcbullard.com When you upload an unlisted video, your subscribers are notified. There's an easy way ...

 How to Insert a Video in Wordpress Widgets Using JW Player
1 week ago · 13 views
How to Insert a Video in Wordpress Widgets Using JW Player ...

YouTube One Channel Tips

YouTube now has the new One Channel Layout. There are new features as well as regular features in different locations. Discover what's new with the One Channel layout and how you can use YouTube's new features t...

 YouTube One Channel Layout - How to Add Channel Artwork, Edit Description, and More
by **Video Marketing for Online Businesses with Marc**
· 1 year ago · 1,128 views
http://www.marcbullard.com YouTube has now opened up the one channel layout to anybody that wants it. Here is ...

 How to edit channel description on YouTube's One Channel Layout
by **Video Marketing for Online Businesses with Marc**
· 1 year ago · 781 views
http://www.topinternetconsulting.com/youtube-marketing-ma... YouTube's new One Channel Layout moves a lot of...

How to send a message to all of your subscribers - YouTube One Channel Layout
by **Video Marketing for Online Businesses with Marc**
· 1 year ago · 13,015 views
http://www.marcbullard.com ATTENTION. THIS METHOD IS NOW DEFUNCT! CLICK HERE TO SEE 2014 TUTORI...

 How to Create New YouTube One Channel Graphic for Free
by **Video Marketing for Online Businesses with Marc**
· 11 months ago · 306 views
http://www.topinternetconsulting.com/youtube-marketing-ma...

The 'Videos' tab will show you a list of your videos and a dropdown box that lets users see individual sections, such as Uploads, Events, Liked Videos, and more.

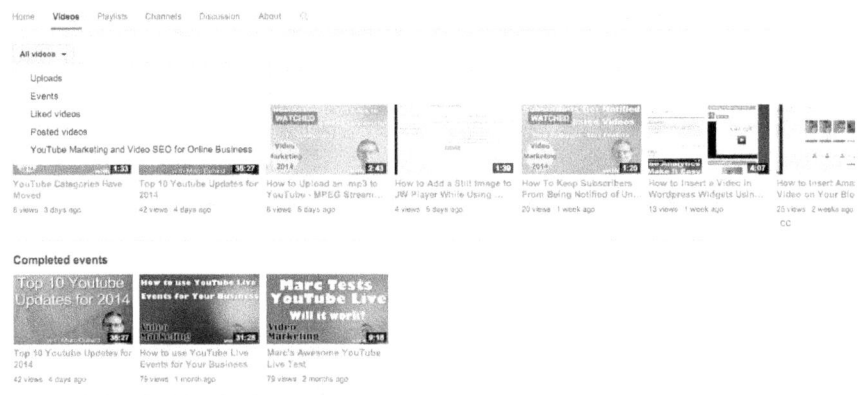

http://www.MarcBullard.com

The 'Playlists' tab shows your created playlists and liked playlists.

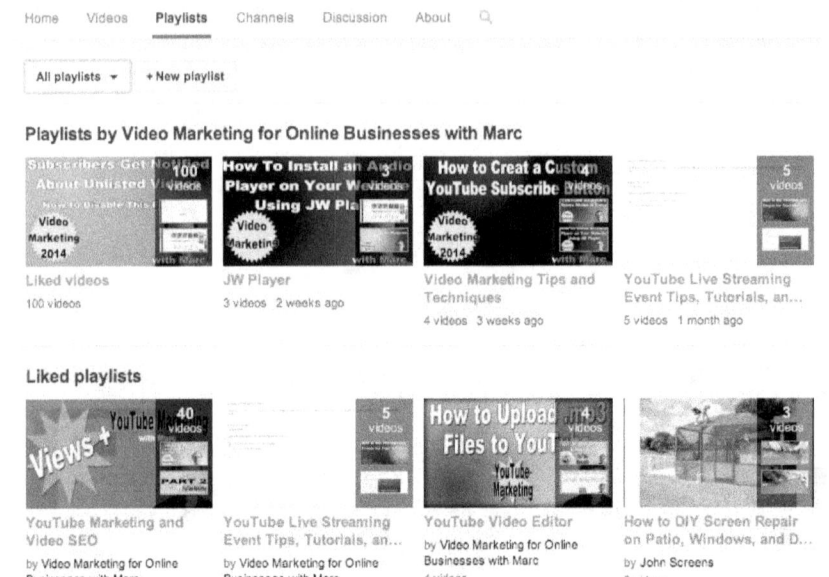

The 'Channels' tab shows visitors other channels you want to feature. These other channels can be channels you have created or others' channels that interest you.

Video Marketing for Online Businesses with Marc

Home   Videos   Playlists   **Channels**   Discussion   About   🔍

Online Business Marketing

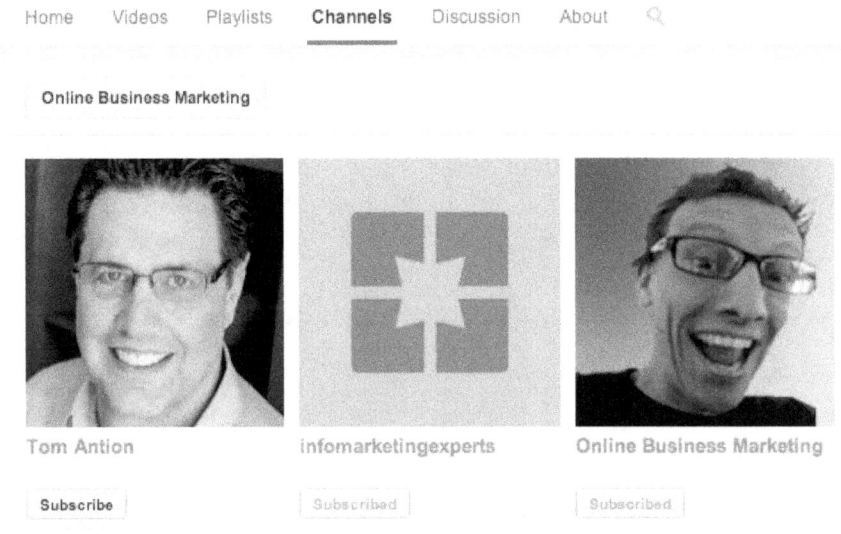

| Tom Antion | infomarketingexperts | Online Business Marketing |
| Subscribe | Subscribed | Subscribed |

The 'Discussion' tab lets you send messages to people visiting your channel. This is a great way to let visitors know about new videos, promote your products, and start conversations.

Video Marketing for Online Businesses with Marc

Home   Videos   Playlists   Channels   **Discussion**   About

ALL COMMENTS (28)

 Share your thoughts

Top comments ∨

 Video Marketing for Online Businesses with Marc   1 month ago
Hi all

Reply ·

 Video Marketing for Online Businesses with Marc   2 months ago
I'm having a new YouTube Live Event Tonight!
How to Use YouTube Live for Your Business
How to use YouTube Live Events for Your Business

Reply · 1

 Video Marketing for Online Businesses with Marc   3 months ago (edited)
New Video on My Business Channel: Webinar Pitches and Closes with Colin Martin.
See it here:
/watch?v=nPmU4WKV9aE

Reply ·

The 'About' tab is probably one of the most important tabs for your YouTube channel when it comes to marketing. The 'About' tab is basically a description area for you YouTube channel.

http://www.MarcBullard.com

Video Marketing for Online Businesses with Marc

Home   Videos   Playlists   Channels   Discussion   **About**

Do you have video marketing questions? Perhaps your small business is looking to start marketing on YouTube? Discover the newest YouTube marketing techniques. Find out what you can do to get your videos discovered by the search engines. New episodes every Tuesday with the latest video marketing tips, YouTube marketing techniques, SEO strategies, and other helpful advice for online businesses.

Who Am I?

With over 14 years experience as a video editor and as a YouTube marketer, I provide video SEO training specifically for YouTube. On top of video production and editing, I consult other online business owners, optimize YouTube channels, create products, and much more

Some of my books include:

YouTube Marketing Handbook

YouTube Marketing Manual

Easy Web Video

Awesome Webinar Method

My Site: MarcBullard.com

Vine Account: YouTubeMarketerMarc

YouTube Channel: http://www.youtube.com/user/videoMTC

⊠ Marc's Website   a YouTube Marketing Manual
⊠ Top Internet Consulting a Easy Web Video Book   510 subscribers
▶ Online Marketing Business   85,849 views

You want to make sure you put information into the 'About' section. This is a great place to tell others about your channel as well as sprinkle in keywords related to your business. Additionally, the 'About' section has an area for you to add links. This is one of three places that YouTube lets users put links so you definitely want to take advantage of it. The 'About' section also shows your Featured Channels and subscriptions (you can turn off the subscriptions if you want).

Channel Editing

Editing your channel lets you determine how you want it to look and what information you want your visitors to be able to see. In order to edit your channel, make sure you're logged in and go to your channel. You can edit different sections of your channel. In order to see if a section is editable, simply hold your mouse over an area and if a pen icon appears, you can edit it.

http://www.MarcBullard.com

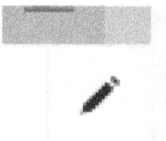

Pen icon means this section is editable.

What section you're in determines what options you have to edit. If you click the pen in the upper right of your channel banner graphic, you will then be able to edit links or channel art.

'Edit links' lets you edit, add, or delete website links in your 'About' section. You can also choose to overlay your first link over your banner graphic if you want.

CUSTOM LINKS   Cancel Done

☑ Overlay first link on channel art

Marc's Website	http://www.marcbullard.com
YouTube Marketing Manual	http://www.amazon.com/gp/product/1482592881/ref=s9_psimh_gw_p14_d2_i1?pf_rd_m=ATVPDKIKX0DER&pf_rd_s:
Top Internet Consulting	http://www.topinternetconsulting.com
Easy Web Video Book	http://www.amazon.com/Easy-Web-Video-Production-ebook/dp/B009KY8JBY/ref=sr_1_1?s=books&ie=UTF8&qid=13
Online Marketing Business	http://www.youtube.com/onlinebizmb

⊕ Add

SOCIAL LINKS

Google+   ▾

☐ Overlay linked G+ page on channel art

Overlay first 1 ▾ social links on channel art

| Google+ | ▾ | https://plus.google.com/u/0/112071134387529412697 |

⊕ Add

STATISTICS

☑ Show views
☑ Show date joined

http://www.MarcBullard.com

Marc's Website
My website overlays my banner graphic.

'Edit channel art' will bring you to a page that lets you upload an image, use a photo you already have, or use a photo from a gallery.

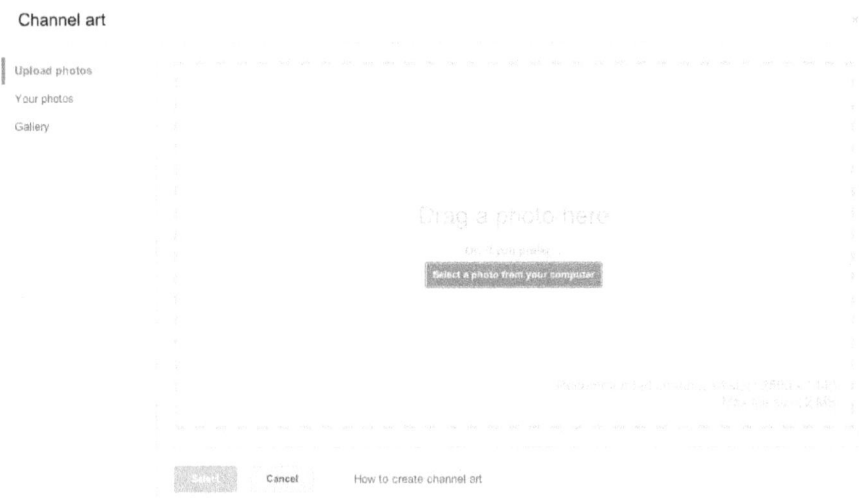

The next editable area is for your channel settings and navigation.

The first option is to edit 'Channel navigation'.

http://www.MarcBullard.com

Channel navigation

🏠 Browse   Default view ✓ Enabled

The Browse view is enabled. Configure it on your channel.

🏠 Feed

You can choose to automatically have your public YouTube activity show up in your channel's activity feed. Don't worry, we'll never share information about activity on private videos.

Post to my activity feed when I...

☐ Add video to public playlist

☐ Like a video or a playlist

☐ Subscribe to a channel

To set the privacy of Likes and Subscriptions, visit your Account Settings

Discussion   ✓ Enabled

Don't display until approved   ▼

Here you can decide to enable/disable the browse view, choose what activity shows up in your feed, and enable/disable the discussion area of your channel. Additionally, you can choose to allow all comments on your channel or approve comments on your channel.

The second link, 'Channel settings' will take you to the advanced area of your channel settings. This was already covered earlier in this book.

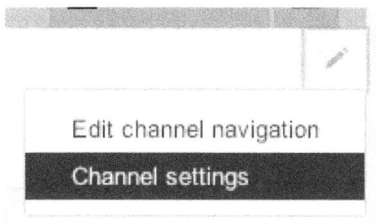

The next editable area on your channel is for your channel trailer.

Below the channel trailer are sections that you get to customize. There are a lot of options for you to choose from and you can have as many sections as you want.

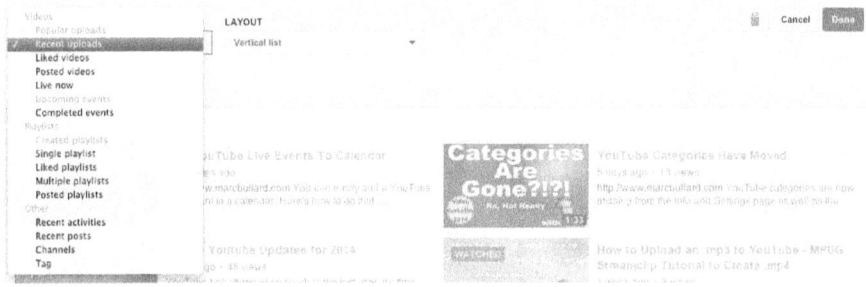

Your sections can contain videos such as 'Recent uploads', 'Liked videos', 'Playlists', 'Posts', 'Channels', and more.

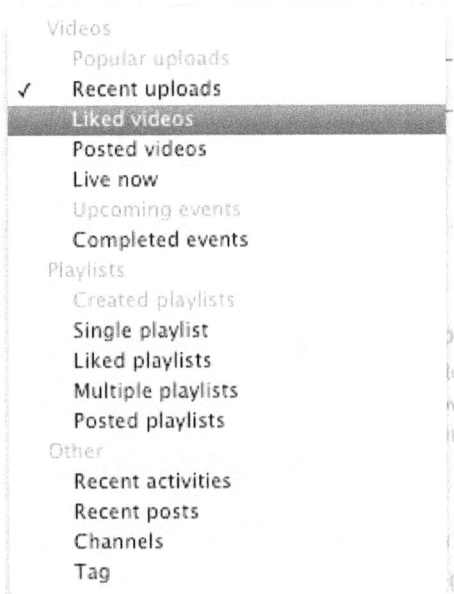

Use these different sections to promote your videos, increase community involvement, promote events, and to fill out your channel. You can also decide on the layout of these sections by choosing either a vertical or horizontal view.

After you've made your selections, be sure to click the 'Done' button and you're all set.

The 'About' section of your channel is extremely important. Not only can you put links to other websites here, but you can also add a description about your channel. This description area should have relevant keywords and provide information about you or your business. To add/edit your 'About' section, click the 'About' tab and hold your mouse over that area.

When you're done editing the 'About' section, click the 'Done' button and you're all set.

Video Editor

Another feature YouTube is giving its users is a video editor. The video editor can be accessed by going into your Video Manager and clicking 'Creation Tools'.

As a video editor for over 14 years now, I have to hand it to them. The video editor does have basic functionality that can be used to make impressive looking videos. When you first access the video editor you will see a place to name your newly edited video, a preview window, tabs for footage, and a timeline.

http://www.MarcBullard.com

The tabs located at the top of the video editor let you access your videos, creative commons videos, audio, transitions, and text.

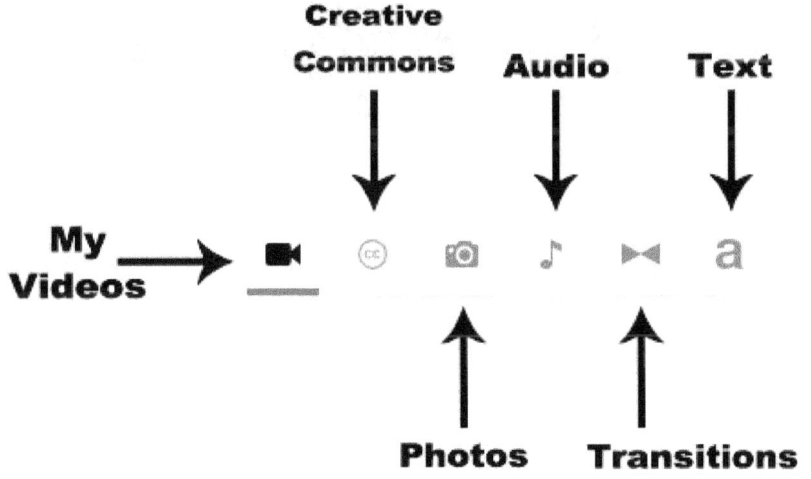

Any video that you have uploaded to YouTube is eligible for you to edit and will be seen in the 'My Videos' tab. Nobody else has access to your videos and the same goes for you with theirs. If what you've uploaded isn't exactly what you need, there are also Creative Commons videos for you and every other YouTube user to choose from.

Remix Creative Commons videos
Search for Creative Commons licensed videos above or check out one of the example videos below. Learn more »

The CC videos are nice and varied with a lot of stock footage style videos.

To add photos to your video, use the 'Photo' tab to select photos from your Google account or upload new images to use.

Add photos to your videos
Select photos from your Google Account, or upload new photos, and insert them into your project.

Add photos to project

To add an audio track, YouTube provides a large list of artists' tracks to choose from.

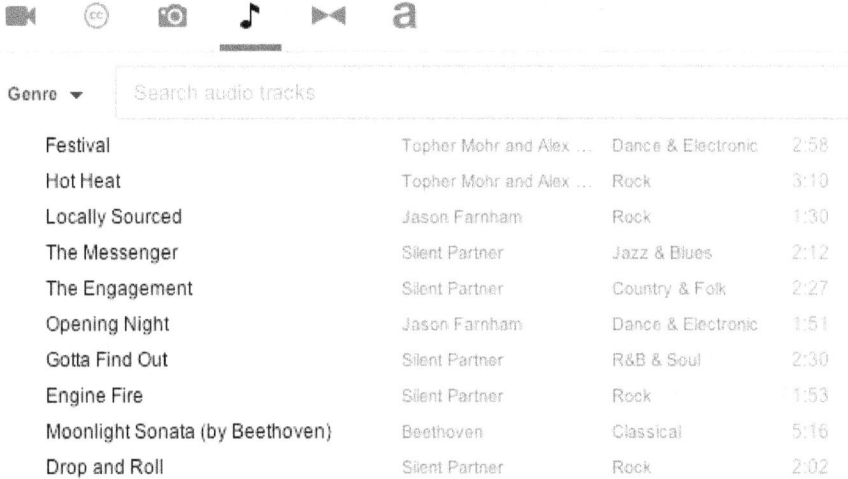

Festival	Topher Mohr and Alex ...	Dance & Electronic	2:58
Hot Heat	Topher Mohr and Alex ...	Rock	3:10
Locally Sourced	Jason Farnham	Rock	1:30
The Messenger	Silent Partner	Jazz & Blues	2:12
The Engagement	Silent Partner	Country & Folk	2:27
Opening Night	Jason Farnham	Dance & Electronic	1:51
Gotta Find Out	Silent Partner	R&B & Soul	2:30
Engine Fire	Silent Partner	Rock	1:53
Moonlight Sonata (by Beethoven)	Beethoven	Classical	5:16
Drop and Roll	Silent Partner	Rock	2:02

How popular and well known these tracks are is beyond me. I didn't recognize any artist available, which means either I'm getting too old or the music selection is coming from lesser known artists. We'll go with the latter for now.

In order to start editing, simply click one of your videos, a creative commons video, or an audio track and drag it into the timeline below.

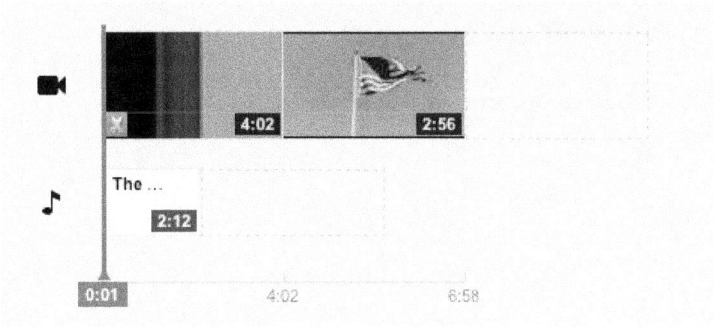

Once you have some video clips in your video timeline, you can then trim them, rotate, and add effects such as making the shot black and white, changing the brightness, and changing the contrast. To trim your clip, options are available when you hover your mouse over that clip.

Clicking on a clip in the timeline will also bring up more options to the right of the preview window.

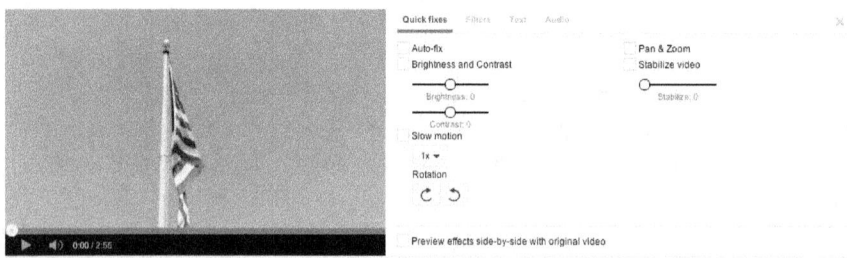

The other options give you tabs for 'Quick fixes', 'Filters', 'Text, and 'Audio'. The 'Quick fixes' tab lets you change the brightnes/contrast, rotate the image, add slow motion and much more.

The 'Filters' tab lets you apply image effects to your video.

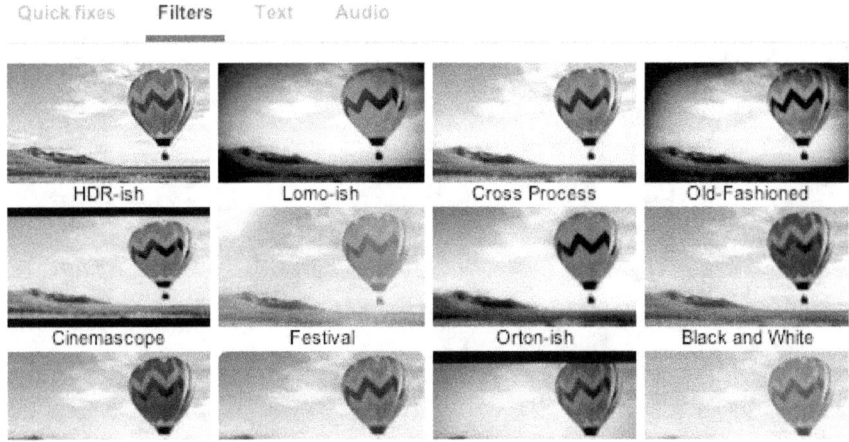

The next tab is to add text.

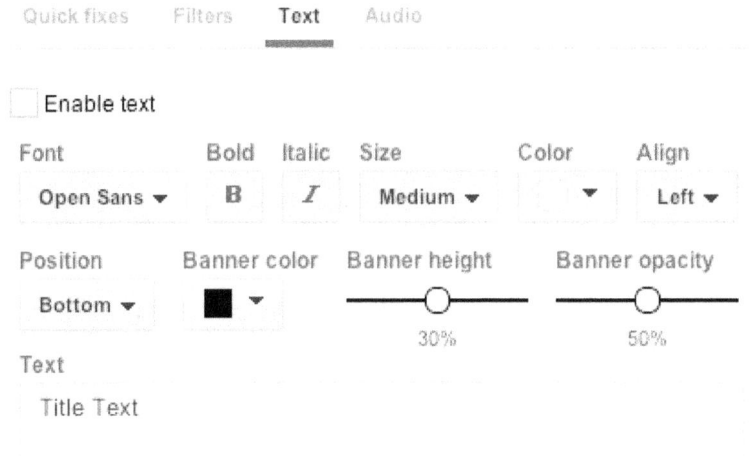

Adding text is pretty simple. Click the 'Enable text' box and then use the other options to customize how you want your text to look.

http://www.MarcBullard.com

The next tab lets you decide how loud you want the audio level to be.

Editing is pretty basic. Each clip has blue handles on the beginning and end of that clip. Dragging these handles lets you shorten or lengthen the video.

http://www.MarcBullard.com

If you want to cut out a section in the middle of a clip, click the scissors that show up when you hover you mouse over that clip. The scissors will turn into a red vertical line that lets you determine where the cut should take place.

 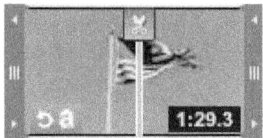

Finally, when you're all done you can name your newly edited project and publish your work back to your YouTube channel. You now have a bright, shiny new video. The original video footage you used for this new video will not be changed.

Feel free to play around with the video editor. It is possible to use this for all of your video editing needs although a standalone editor that's on your computer might be easier to use in the long run.

YouTube Analytics

Attempting to get traffic, views, and comments from your videos but not tracking your efforts' progress is a huge shot in the foot. You should always be comparing and contrasting what efforts you made and what results you achieved from them. Analytics is just the tool for that.

YouTube Analytics is an extremely powerful set of tools that can provide you with a lot of information about your videos, your audience, and your customers.

To access Analytics, click your username in the upper right hand corner and select 'Video Manager' from the drop down list. In your video manager, there are links in the left menu. One of them is the 'Analytics' link.

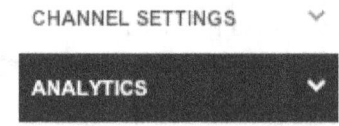

Clicking on 'Analytics' will bring you to the Overview page.

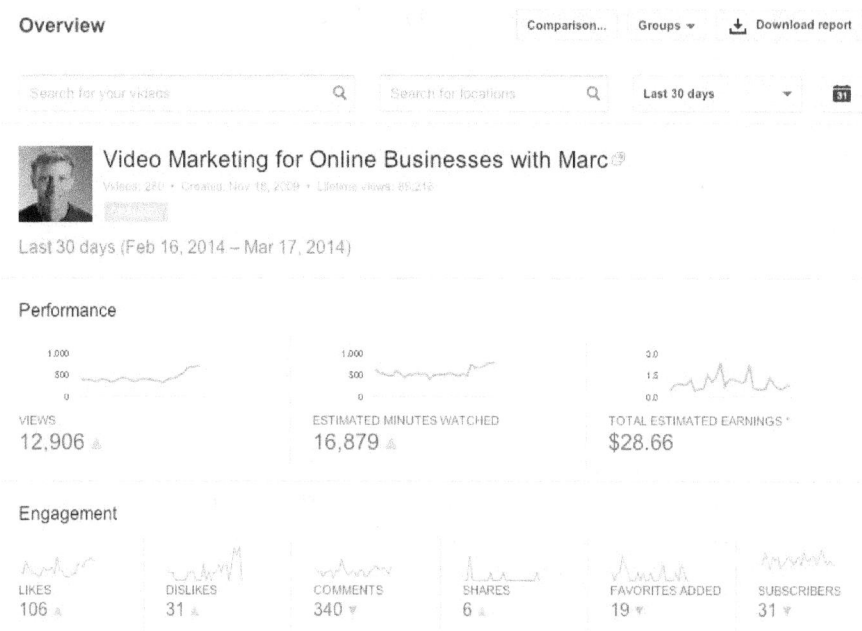

The Overview page consists of a menu on the left hand side. This page provides high level modules such as 'Performance', 'Engagement', 'Top 10 videos' and more. You can also compare videos to each other, group videos together, and download a report, all located at the top of the page. The default date range is the last 30 days.

The large middle section of the Overview page will provide you with some of the most used widgets. The smaller, left hand section also contains these widgets but in a different order. This left hand section breaks down the widgets into three large sections: **EARNINGS REPORTS, VIEWS REPORTS,** and **ENGAGEMENT REPORTS.**

Data Filters are available for all reports. This lets you search for content, such as a specific video; geography, such as a certain country; or by date range. You can check these numbers by daily, weekly, monthly, yearly, or custom metrics. Using data filters will change the results on your overview page.

Each section - called widgets - is click-able. When you click on a widget, you get your reports for that section. Also, every report that is provided to you is available to download for your records. Once clicked, you will receive a .csv file you can keep in a spreadsheet or print out.

The first widget available on the overview page is for 'Views'. It is located under a larger **Performance** category. Clicking on the 'Views' widget will bring up more details concerning your views.

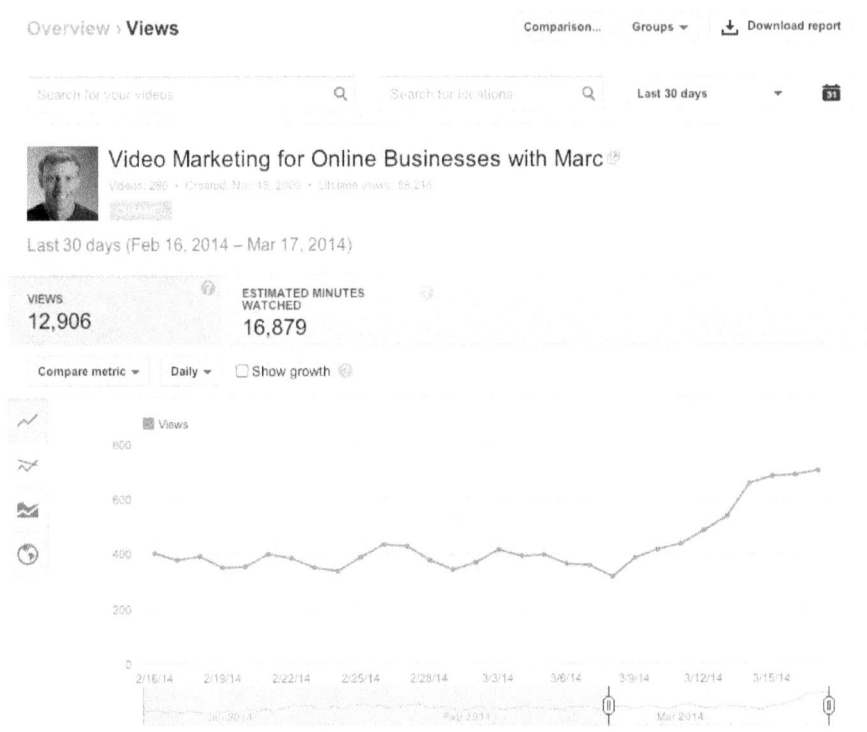

You will be able to see your videos listed by views as well as geographical information and dates. In order to access geographical information or dates, click on the corresponding tab.

http://www.MarcBullard.com

	Video Geography Date			
	Geography	Views ↓	Monetizable views	Estimated minutes watched
1.	United States	54,099	29,024	39,171
2.	United Kingdom	10,374	6,381	6,693
3.	Canada	5,681	3,348	4,516
4.	India	3,817	2,601	2,671
5.	Australia	3,679	2,196	2,604
6.	Philippines	3,500	2,374	2,203
7.	Malaysia	2,118	1,541	1,447
8.	Germany	1,394	705	513
9.	Netherlands	1,299	762	425
10.	Brazil	1,105	681	292
11.	Indonesia	1,019	685	467
12.	Pakistan	948	646	51
13.	Ireland	934	567	565
14.	Romania	917	648	295
15.	Singapore	902	583	526
16.	Mexico	885	557	447
17.	Greece	867	498	431
18.	Sweden	823	486	398
19.	Italy	752	492	257
20.	Portugal	729	457	353

Geography tab.

	Video Geography Date				
	Date ↓	Views	Monetizable views	Unique cookies	Estimated minutes watched
1.	Jan 28, 2013	211	128	190	570
2.	Jan 27, 2013	199	155	174	410
3.	Jan 26, 2013	203	148	173	384
4.	Jan 25, 2013	233	165	197	753
5.	Jan 24, 2013	214	141	169	481
6.	Jan 23, 2013	244	167	212	591
7.	Jan 22, 2013	205	129	176	473
8.	Jan 21, 2013	206	140	176	414
9.	Jan 20, 2013	216	143	176	505

Date tab.

The default chart of your views is a line chart. You can also see a multi line chart, stacked area chart, and map.

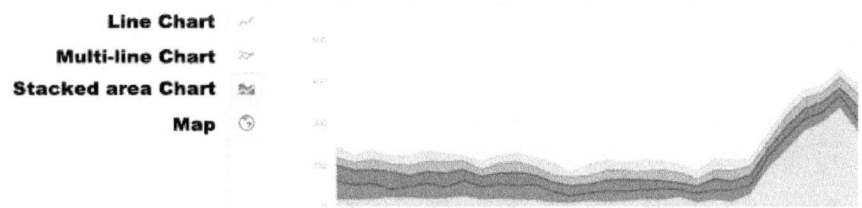

You can also compare different metrics within the charts.

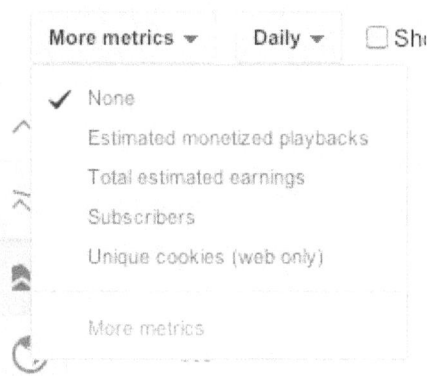

All of these results are important to pay attention to. First, you can use this information to determine what countries are interested in your video. If you find that more people are watching your video from Brazil, it might make sense to translate your captions or transcript into Portuguese; thereby capturing an even larger audience from that country. You should also pay attention to the dates that views either increase or decrease. Of course views are going to fluctuate, but if you notice a large difference between particular days you may want to make a note of anything that could have caused that large fluctuation, such as whether it was a weekend, holiday, you made a change in tags on that day, etc.

Not only can you see your views with a line graph, you can also see them by geographical location. Clicking the 'Map' button will provide you with a map of the world. Holding your mouse over any area will give you the number of views that came from that area.

*In Russia, views count **you**!*

Back on the Overview Page, the next widget under the **Performance** category is for 'Estimated Minutes Watched'.

Clicking this will show you a graph that outlines minutes watched on certain dates.

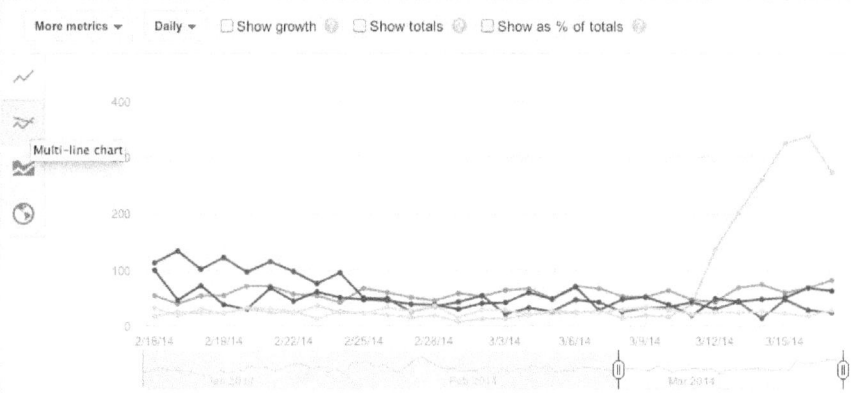

As with all other widgets, you can see stats as a Line Chart or as a Map. Also, you can change the information by date or other metrics.

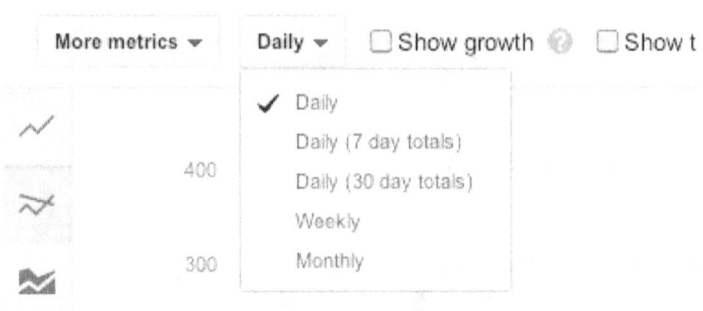

Sort by date range

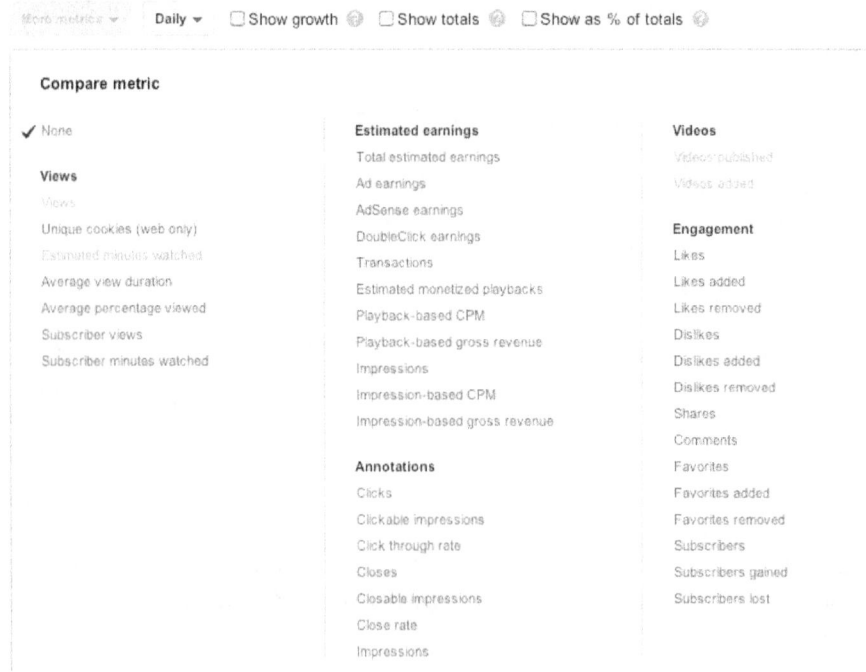

Sort by other metrics

http://www.MarcBullard.com

Viewing the graph as a Map will show you analytics on what locations account for the most minutes watched.

On the main Overview page, the next widget is 'Total Estimated Earnings' or 'Subscribers'. You will have the first option if you chose to monetize your videos. If not, you will see the second choice: 'Subscribers'. 'Subscribers' is moved down to the next category of the Overview page: **Engagement**.

ATCHED

TOTAL ESTIMATED EARNINGS *

$28.66

* These earnings are only estimates. Earnings data can take up to seven days to appear. If you see
a day within the last seven that is showing no earnings, even if there is a later day with earnings,
please check back again tomorrow.

Back on the 'Overview' page, you will see widgets for the **Engagement**
category. Engagement widgets cover 'Likes', 'Dislikes', 'Comments',
'Shares', 'Favorites added', and 'Favorites removed'.

Engagement

LIKES	DISLIKES	COMMENTS	SHARES	FAVORITES ADDED	SUBSCRIBERS
106	31	340	6	19	31

Clicking the 'Like' widget will bring you to that report page.

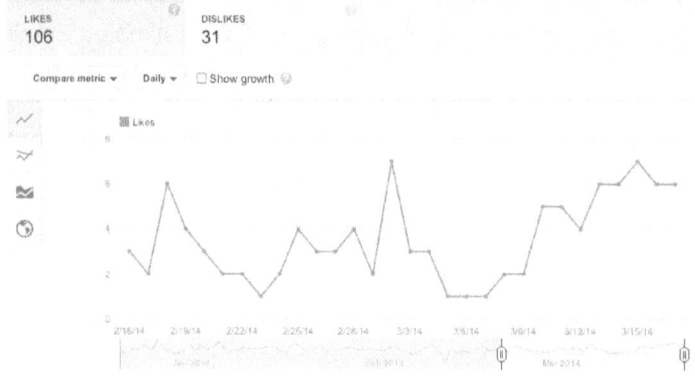

This report page has all of the same options as 'Views', 'Subscribers', and others, so there's no need to go over every option you can use. However, there is one metric that hasn't been covered yet, and that is the 'Compare metric'.

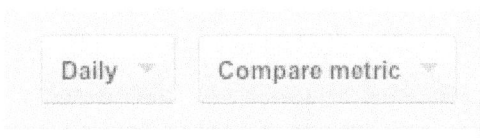

The 'Compare metric' will let you see extra information displayed on your line chart. It's not available for every report, but for the reports that do have it, the metric will be a little different.

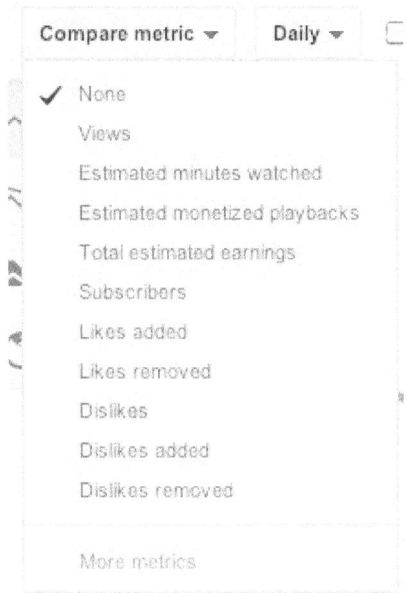

Compare metric for 'Likes' and 'Dislikes'.

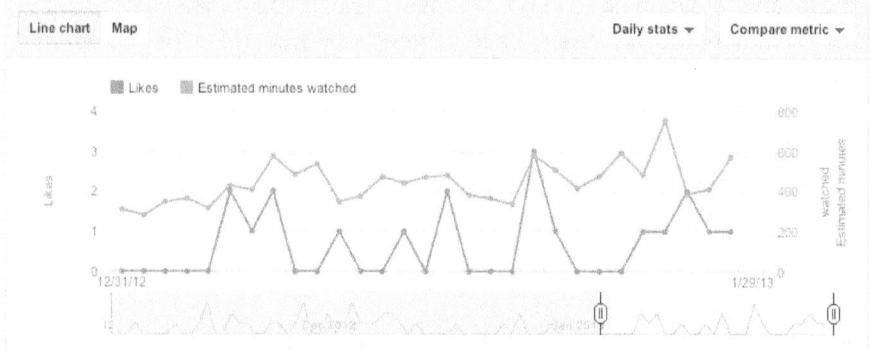

Choosing a compare metric will display extra information.

You can see reports and their compare metrics for your entire YouTube channel or for individual videos.

On the Overview page, below the **Engagement** category, you will see a list of your **Top 10 Videos.**

Top 10 Videos   Browse as content

Video	Views ↓	Estimated minutes watched	Total estimated earnings
How to Turn Off 'Use YouTube As' Screen W...	2,035	2,046	$1.34
How to Upload an MP3 to YouTube - Great fo...	1,364	1,464	$3.64
How to send a message to all of your subscri...	1,172	1,687	$3.91
How To Upload .mp3 Files to YouTube	999	1,747	$1.99
How to Add Formatting to YouTube Comment...	948	761	$0.64
How To Send a Message To Your Subscriber...	687	842	$0.86
How to edit your audio track in Garageband	340	563	$0.85
How to fade in and fade out audio track in Ga...	330	399	$0.70
How To Read, Edit, and Delete YouTube Co...	312	292	$0.43
How to find Tags of any YouTube Video - Gre...	252	330	$0.56

The top 10 videos are listed in order of views. You can also choose to browse all of your videos.

Browse all content		
Videos Shows Groups	Search for content	Search
Video	Upload date	Lifetime views
How to send a message to all of your subscribers - YouTube One Channel Layout	Mar 18, 2013	13,122
How to Upload an MP3 to YouTube - Great for YouTube's New Audio Library and Video Editor	Mar 8, 2013	9,403
How to fade in and fade out audio track in GarageBand	Dec 5, 2012	4,902
How to Turn Off 'Use YouTube As' Screen When Logging In - YouTube Channel Selector	Oct 24, 2013	4,156
How to Add Formatting to YouTube Comments - Bold, Italics, and Strikethroughs...Oh my.	Sep 26, 2013	4,019
YouTube Pause Annotation - Gone, but Not Really	Apr 4, 2013	3,358
How to Make CD and DVD Labels for Free	Feb 12, 2013	2,715
How To Upload .mp3 Files to YouTube	Jan 8, 2014	2,346
How to edit your audio track in GarageBand	Dec 5, 2012	2,289
How to find Tags of any YouTube Video - Great for Video Keyword Research	Dec 21, 2012	2,017
How to Share Private YouTube Videos with Specific People, emails, and Circles	Jul 2, 2013	2,005
Remove That Feed - How to change default YouTube channel page	May 13, 2013	1,614
How to turn off and disable all annotations on YouTube videos	Apr 24, 2013	1,611
How to Disable the Discussion Tab on Your YouTube Channel	May 30, 2013	1,584
How to turn off (disable) related channels on YouTube	May 3, 2013	1,458
		1 - 15 of many Next

When browsing all of your content, you can arrange the results by 'Upload date' or 'Lifetime views'. Clicking on any title of a video will give you an overview page for only that video.

Below the **Top 10 videos** category is the **Demographics** category. This category can provide you with some valuable information about who is watching your videos.

http://www.MarcBullard.com

Clicking the 'Top geographies' widget will show you what countries are providing the most views. A list of the countries in order of views will also be available.

1.	United States	2.603
2.	United Kingdom	456
3.	Canada	298
4.	Australia	193
5.	Philippines	124
6.	India	116
7.	Malaysia	92
8.	Netherlands	70
9.	Brazil	66
10.	Norway	58
11.	Germany	56
12.	Greece	47
13.	Pakistan	42
14.	Italy	42
15.	Singapore	41
16.	Indonesia	38
17.	Sweden	37
18.	Romania	36
19.	Mexico	36
20.	Poland	35
21.	Thailand	33
22.	Hong Kong	33
23.	Ireland	33
24.	Portugal	32
25.	Israel	31

Clicking on the name of a country will show you information on only that country.

http://www.MarcBullard.com

Clicking the 'Video' tab for that country will show you the exact videos that received views from that country.

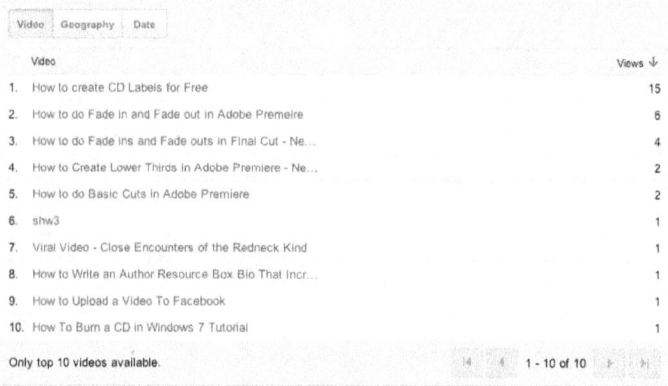

If you find a country that likes a particular video, you may want to create one tailored specifically for that country, or at least add transcripts in that country's language to increase even more views.

The next widget in the **Demographics** category is for gender.

Clicking on this widget will provide you with gender, age, and location information about your viewers.

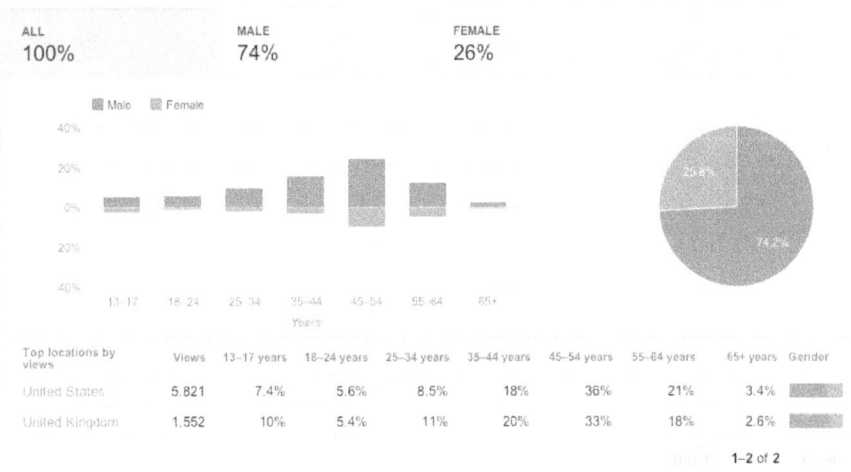

Pay attention to this information. If you have a particular video that is getting a lot of attention from a specific gender, location, or age group, you may want to create more videos like that one. Also, if you have a product or

http://www.MarcBullard.com

service that fits a specific demographic, this will let you know what videos are reaching your desired audience.

The **Discovery** category contains two very useful widgets, 'Top playback locations' and 'Top traffic sources'.

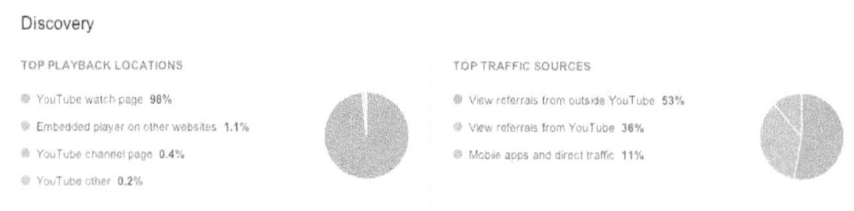

'Top playback locations' will show you a graph with information on your views and where they are coming from.

The Playback location will tell you where your views are coming from. The 'YouTube watch page' is when people view your video on a regular YouTube page. The location entitled "Embedded player on other websites" won't tell you what the other sites are unless you are looking at the locations for specific videos.

Playback location*	Views ↓	Estimated minutes watched	Average view duration
YouTube watch page	1,358 (100%)	1,457 (100%)	1:04
Embedded player on other websites	5 (0.4%)	7 (0.5%)	1:22
YouTube other	1 (0.1%)	0 (0.0%)	0:00
			1–3 of 3

Playback location for a specific video.

If you look at the Playback location reports for a specific video, you can click on the "Embedded player on other websites" link to see where that video is embedded.

Top level ▸ **Embedded player on other websites**

Playback location   Geography   Date

Playback location	Views ↓	Estimated minutes watched	Average view duration
mail.google.com	2 (40%)	5 (67%)	2:18
softpedia.com	2 (40%)	2 (28%)	0:57
unknown	1 (20%)	0 (5.3%)	0:22

Looking at the other websites your video is embedded on will let you know exactly where your video is playing. Also, you may find sites that you could contact and try to send more videos to, or offer other options such as submitting articles for them or placing a banner ad on their site. This can increase traffic to your site and increase sales of your products.

http://www.MarcBullard.com

Back on the main **Overview** page, the 'Top traffic sources' widget is also very helpful, it is located under the **Discovery** category.

TOP TRAFFIC SOURCES

- View referrals from outside YouTube 51%

- View referrals from YouTube 41%

- Mobile apps and direct traffic 8.8%

This widget will show you how people discovered your video. There's many ways people find videos: they search for them on YouTube, Google, or other search engines; they click on Suggested videos, or they can follow links from social networking sites such as Twitter or Facebook. Also, there is information for mobile apps.

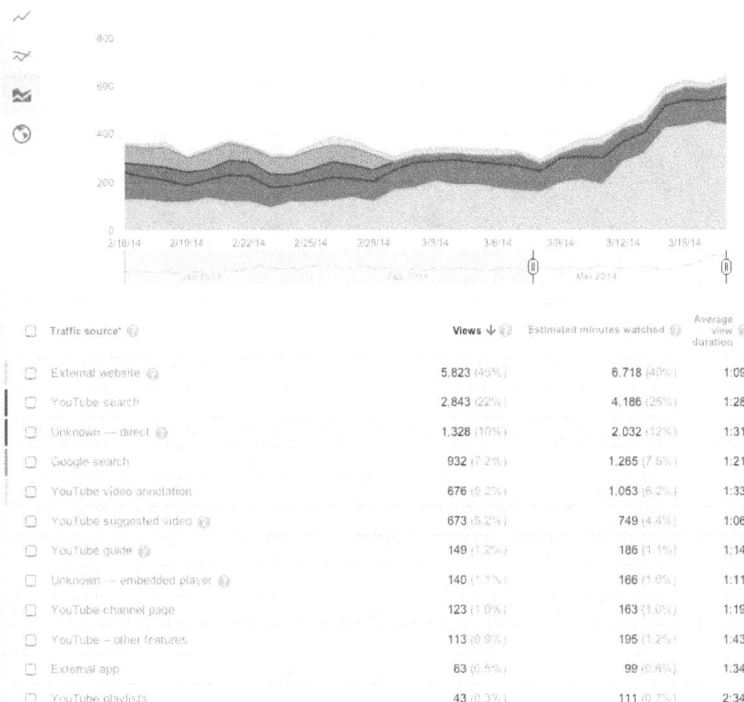

Traffic source	Views ↓	Estimated minutes watched	Average view duration
External website	5,823 (45%)	6,718 (40%)	1:09
YouTube search	2,843 (22%)	4,186 (25%)	1:28
Unknown — direct	1,328 (10%)	2,032 (12%)	1:31
Google search	932 (7.2%)	1,265 (7.5%)	1:21
YouTube video annotation	676 (5.2%)	1,053 (6.2%)	1:33
YouTube suggested video	673 (5.2%)	749 (4.4%)	1:06
YouTube guide	149 (1.2%)	186 (1.1%)	1:14
Unknown — embedded player	140 (1.1%)	166 (1.0%)	1:11
YouTube channel page	123 (1.0%)	163 (1.0%)	1:19
YouTube – other features	113 (0.9%)	195 (1.2%)	1:43
External app	63 (0.5%)	99 (0.6%)	1:34
YouTube playlists	43 (0.3%)	111 (0.7%)	2:34

Traffic sources for entire channel.

The traffic sources can be displayed for either your whole channel or individual videos. Individual videos will provide you with even more information.

☐ External website	536 (39%)	517 (35%)	0:57
☐ YouTube search	524 (38%)	636 (43%)	1:12
☐ Google search	152 (11%)	136 (9.3%)	0:53
☐ Unknown — direct	116 (8.5%)	144 (9.8%)	1:14
☐ YouTube suggested video	19 (1.4%)	13 (0.9%)	0:39
☐ YouTube – other features	6 (0.4%)	10 (0.7%)	1:40
☐ YouTube channel page	4 (0.3%)	1 (0.1%)	0:17
☐ Unknown — embedded player	4 (0.3%)	7 (0.4%)	1:37
☐ External app	2 (0.1%)	2 (0.1%)	0:59
☐ YouTube guide	1 (0.1%)	2 (0.1%)	1:48

Traffic sources for individual videos. Note: 'YouTube suggested video' and other links are now click-able.

When you look at traffic sources for individual videos, some of those sources will be click-able. If it is available for your particular video, the 'YouTube suggested video' link is extremely useful.

☐ Traffic source	Views ↓	Estimated minutes watched	Average view duration
☐ How to Upload an MP3 to YouTube - Great for ...	13 (68%)	9 (69%)	0:39
☐ Upload MP3 to YouTube Free [How-To]	2 (11%)	3 (24%)	1:31
☐ How to Upload Music to Youtube (MP3,WMA)	1 (5.3%)	0 (0.6%)	0:04
☐ Etege Taitu Bitul	1 (5.3%)	0 (1.9%)	0:13
☐ How To Upload .mp3 Files to YouTube	1 (5.3%)	0 (2.0%)	0:14
☐ how to use Youtube Video Editor add audio	1 (5.3%)	0 (2.7%)	0:19

Clicking on this link will show you other people's videos that had yours in the suggested videos column on the right hand side of YouTube.

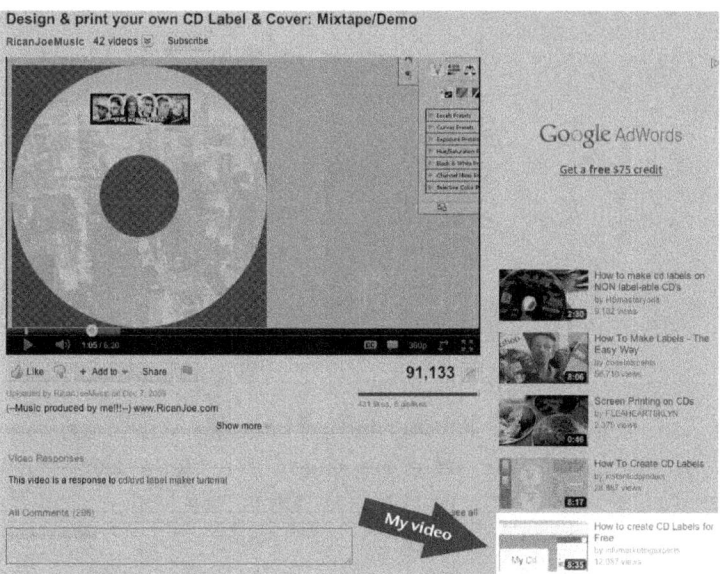

This means people went to this video first, then saw mine in the suggested videos column and clicked on that. If I want to increase my views from this other person's video, I might go and add comments or video responses to their video, possibly even suggesting to others that they will find additional or helpful information in my video. I can do this for every video that shows up in my traffic source list.

Your traffic source list may show that you got views from Google or YouTube search as well.

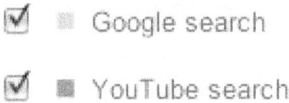

Clicking on these links will provide you with a list of search terms people typed in that resulted in them clicking your video.

http://www.MarcBullard.com

Traffic source	Views ↓	Estimated minutes watched	Average view duration
how to upload audio on youtube	94 (18%)	108 (17%)	1:08
how to upload mp3 on youtube	31 (5.9%)	42 (6.6%)	1:20
unknown	29 (5.5%)	51 (8.0%)	1:45
upload audio to youtube	21 (4.0%)	21 (3.3%)	1:00
how to upload audio file on youtube	17 (3.2%)	14 (2.2%)	0:49
how to upload a mp3 on youtube	15 (2.9%)	19 (2.9%)	1:14
how to upload mp3 to youtube	15 (2.9%)	15 (2.3%)	0:58
how to upload a audio on youtube	13 (2.5%)	22 (3.4%)	1:39
how to upload a audio file to youtube	12 (2.3%)	5 (0.9%)	0:27

You can look at these search terms and get ideas for other videos (or articles) you may want to create in the future. Creating more content with these search terms will show you as an expert in your field, adding credibility to your business and getting additional views as well.

In the left menu under 'Views reports', you will see 'Devices'.

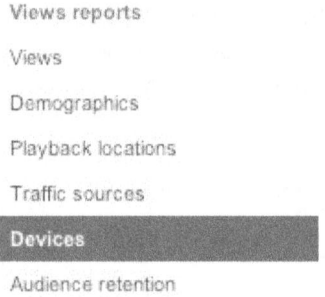

This will bring up a page that shows what device your viewers are watching your video on.

Device type	Views ↓	Estimated minutes watched	Average view duration
Computer	1,218 (89%)	1,227 (84%)	1:00
Mobile phone	91 (6.7%)	153 (11%)	1:40
Tablet	55 (4.0%)	95 (6.5%)	1:44

This can be very helpful. For example, if you see that a lot of viewers are watching your videos on mobile phones or tablets you may want to take into consideration that screens on those devices are smaller than a computer. This means that graphics and text may be harder to read so you can prepare for that on future videos. Also, phones and tablets don't show annotations, just another thing you may want to be prepared for.

Another link in the left menu is for 'Audience retention'.

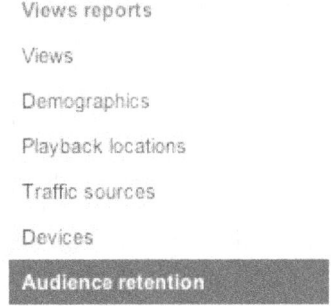

Audience retention refers to the amount of time viewers are staying on your video. This is extremely important. YouTube is paying attention to the amount of time viewers stay watching your videos and will base search rankings on this. When you click 'Audience retention' you will see a page with your video as well as a line graph.

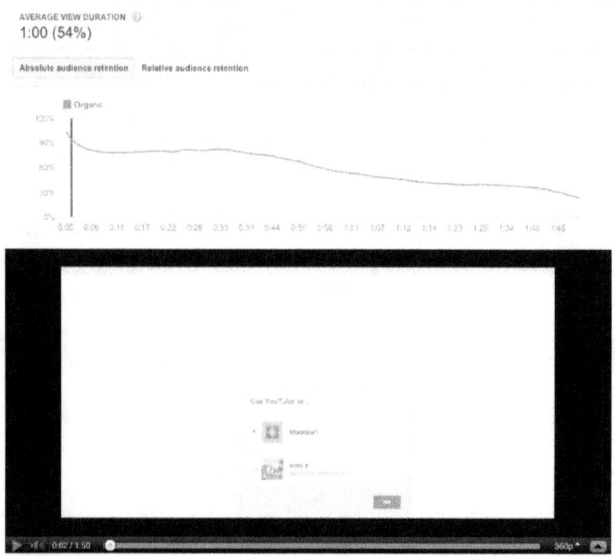

The line graph shows the amount of viewers watching your video at that particular time in the actual video. If you look at the line graph, you will see the number of viewers drops the farther through the video you go. This means that if you have important information in the last ten seconds of your video, only a fraction of the viewers are seeing it compared to the first ten seconds. You may want to create new video content with this in mind. The same thing goes for annotations, calls to action, and anything else that you want viewers to be aware of. Now, if you look closer at the line graph you will see that near the beginning of the video you might actually have more than 100% of viewers watching your video. How can this be?

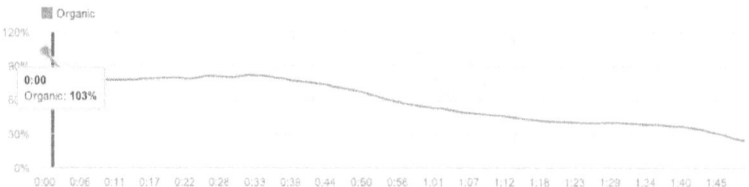

http://www.MarcBullard.com

You can get more than 100% retention if viewers rewind the video and watch a certain section again. You may also see sections of the graph that go up instead of down. This is also where viewers are backing the video up and watching it again.

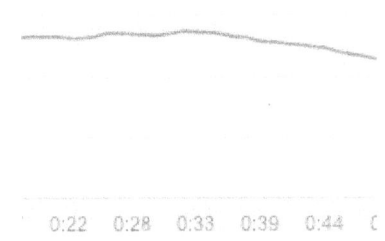

0:22   0:28   0:33   0:39   0:44   0

This too, is important to pay attention to. This section of the video must have had something in it that viewers wanted to watch again. It could be for multiple reasons too: maybe it was confusing, helpful, funny, etc. Once you figure out why they were backing up at this point, you may be able to create similar videos, add annotations, add graphics, or any number of things to capitalize on this section of video.

Analytics Conclusion

That's all of the features of YouTube's analytics. Don't let it scare you, it is provided to help you and your business. Poke around all of the features and use this guide to help you pinpoint where, how, and why you're getting views. Then make more videos and do it all over again, probably with better results, thanks to the information you now know how to get and use. When you are first starting out, analytics may not provide any useful information. The numbers tell more of a story the longer your videos are out there getting views.

Analysis and Research Tools

Oddly enough, a lot of businesses large and small aren't using all of the free services YouTube offers to increase, analyze, and target traffic. I have outlined some of the most important and highly overlooked features YouTube provides for all of its members.

YouTube Trends - *http://youtube-trends.blogspot.com/*

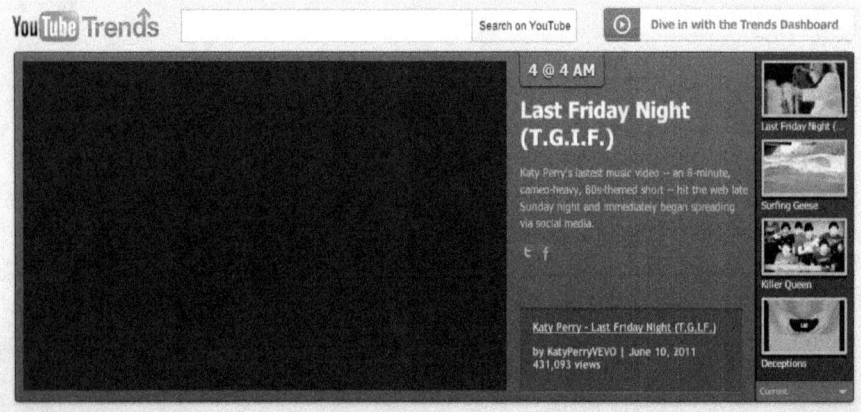

YouTube Trends is a site created by YouTube to showcase the latest videos and trends that are currently popular on their site. YouTube Trends is made for anybody who wants to know what's popular on YouTube at any given moment. The site offers you a couple of categories that break down the information such as 'Popular Videos, 'Popular on the Web', and '4 at 4'.

'4 at 4' are videos that are creating significant buzz on YouTube and other sites.

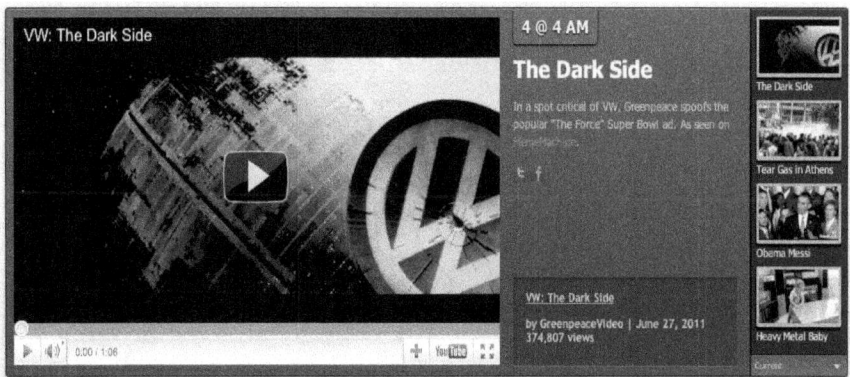

Every 4am and 4pm Eastern time, YouTube Trends identifies the top 4 videos at that time. '4 at 4' is a great way to see the most recent popular happenings at the time. This is a great way to find out what's new right away.

You can view the trending videos for each category as well.

Categories

- Advertising
- Community
- Culture
- Gaming
- Holidays
- Local
- Movies
- Music
- Newsroom
- Politics
- Search
- Sports
- Technology
- Viral
- Weather
- World

Trends Dashboard - *http://www.youtube.com/trendsdashboard*

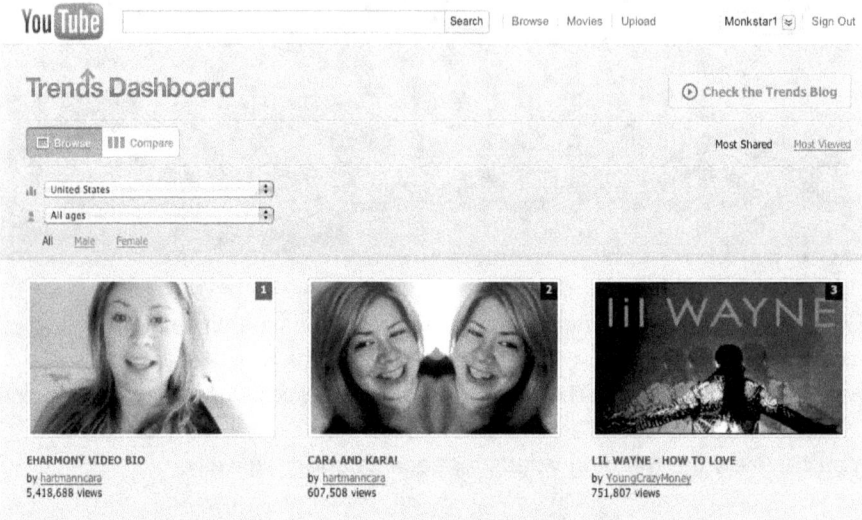

One of the best and often overlooked features of YouTube Trends is the 'Trends Dashboard'. Located at the top of the YouTube Trends website, the Dashboard opens up more tools to help you figure out a wealth of information. To access this, click the 'Dive in with the trends' button.

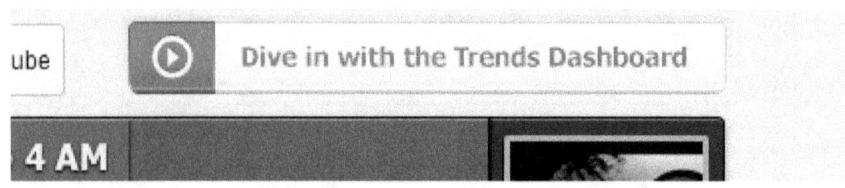

The Trends Dashboard let's you look at the most viewed and most shared videos.

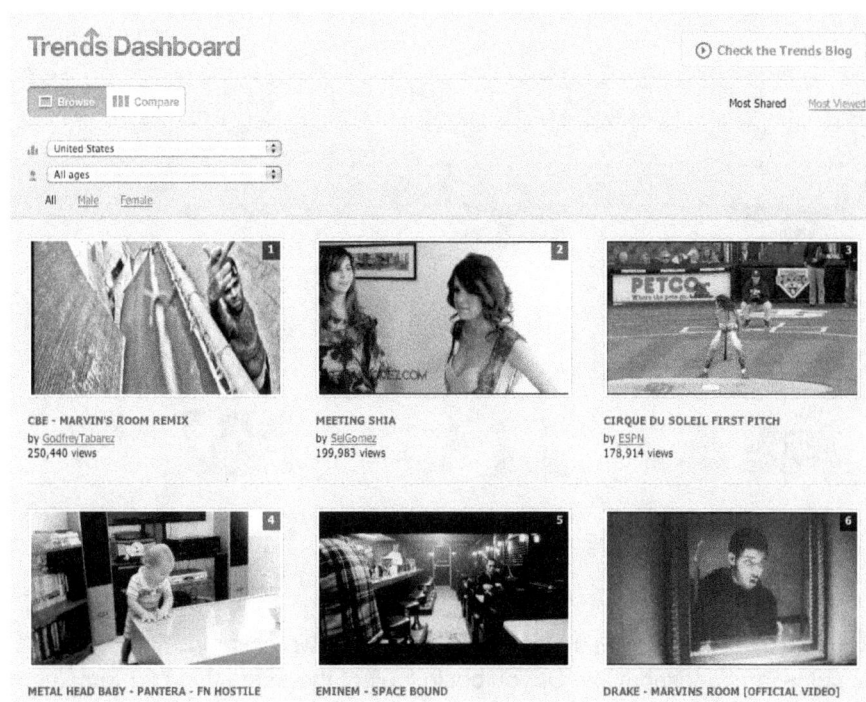

You can browse them with different options such as location by city, gender, and age demographic. This means you could find out what the most viewed videos by females aged 18-24 are in the Baltimore, MD area. Or you can view what both genders are watching in the 55-64 age group.

The Dashboard even offers up the option to compare multiple search parameters.

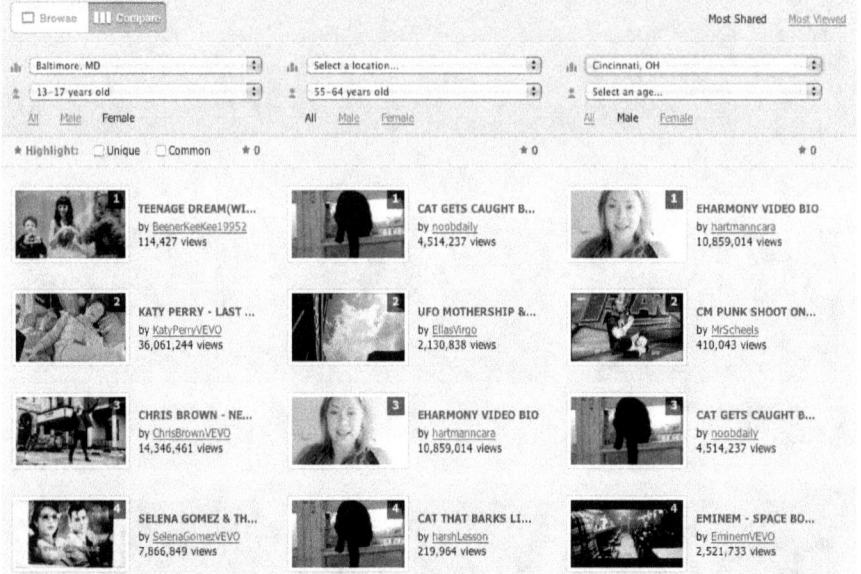

You could compare what males, aged 25-34, are watching in Cincinnati, Los Angeles, and Jacksonville. Or you could look at the same thing for females. The options are endless. Once you know what your target audience is looking for, you can create and market videos of the same type, style, length, etc.

Google Trends – http://www.google.com/trends
Google Trends shows how often a particular search-term is entered relative to the total search-volume across various regions of the world, and in various languages.

You can use Google Trends to see what hot issues are popular at the moment. This site is updated every day so you can always find new information about what people are searching for. Now, if you find something on Google Trends that you can related to your business, you can create a video on that subject and ride off of the popularity of those keywords. This is a great way to get new ideas for videos.

Google Alerts – http://www.google.com/alerts
A great way to stay up to date on topics that are related to your content is to use Google Alerts. Google Alerts are email updates of the latest relevant Google results (web, news, etc.) based on your queries.

http://www.MarcBullard.com

Search query:

Result type: Everything

Language: English

Region: Any Region

How often: Once a day

How many: Only the best results

Deliver to: Bullard.Marc@gmail.com

CREATE ALERT   Manage your alerts

All you need to do is type in a word (usually one of your keywords) in the Search query box. Pick the other settings from the dropdown boxes and enter your email address. Now, you will be emailed whenever information related to your query come up online. This is a great way to stay up to date on the newest things happening. Then, if you can think of a way to create a video using this information you will be one of the first people to do so.

YouTube URL and Embed Tricks

Here are a few neat URL tricks you can use with your videos.

http://www.MarcBullard.com

Start your video playing at any time you specify

Let's say you have a video that's 3 minutes long but the good stuff doesn't begin until a minute in. Simply add '**#t=XXmYYs**' (don't use the quotes ') to the share URL. In the example, XX stands for minutes, and YY stands for seconds. So, if I wanted my video to start a minute in, I would add the code '**#t=01m00s**' to the end of the URL.

View in High Quality

When you provide a link to a video, you have the option to have the link be a high quality version of the video. All you have to do is place a little bit more code at the end of your shared video URL. Simply add '**&fmt=22**' (don't use the quotes ') to the end.

Embed in High Quality

While trick number 1 works for the share link, it won't work with embedded videos. In order to show your embedded video in high quality, simply add '**&ap=%2526fmt%3D22**' (don't use the quotes ').

Autoplay an embedded video

Normally when you embed a video on a site, the player will sit on the site waiting for somebody to hit play. In order to have your video start the instant somebody goes to that page, you simply add the code '**&autoplay=1**' (don't use the quotes ') to the URL. This is also a good way to increase views because every time somebody visits your site, the video starts playing, counting as another view.

Add code here

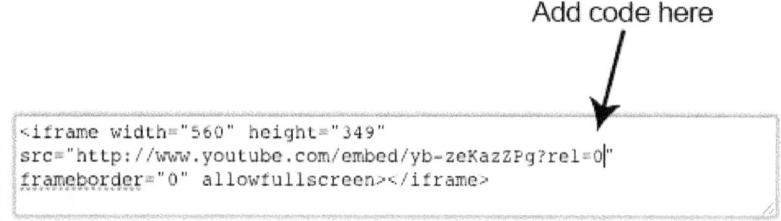

```
<iframe width="560" height="349"
src="http://www.youtube.com/embed/yb-zeKazZPg?rel=0"
frameborder="0" allowfullscreen></iframe>
```

For all of the embed code examples, add the extra code at the end of the video URL. In this case, the URL is http://www.youtube.com/embed/yb-zeKazZPG?rel=0.

Loop an embedded video
If you would like to loop a video so once it finishes, it'll start over again, simply add **'&loop=1'** (don't use quotes ')

Remove the YouTube Logo from the Player with Modest Branding
YouTube now allows the player to contain no YouTube logo, they call this Modest Branding. Take a look at the pictures below.

YouTube Logo

When you embed a video on your site, YouTube normally has a small logo in the bottom right of the player. The problem with this is that for some serious businesses, the logo bothers them and so they won't use YouTube for their embedding needs. What YouTube has done is made it easier for businesses to use the YouTube player on their sites by giving them the option to remove the logo.

In order to remove the YouTube logo from the player, all you have to do is insert a small bit of code in the video's embed code. The small bit of code looks like this:

?modestbranding=1

Usually, the embed code looks like this:

<iframe width="560" height="349" src="http://www.youtube.com/embed/7ZNFLFHhPWc?rel=0" frameborder="0" allowfullscreen></iframe>

This embed code will create a player that has the logo. What you need to do is put in the small extra bit of code so it looks like this:

<iframe width="560" height="349" src="http://www.youtube.com/embed/7ZNFLFHhPWc**?modestbranding=1** " frameborder="0" allowfullscreen></iframe>

I put in bold where the code needs to be inserted; your code will not be bolded.

Once you put the extra code in, your video will look like this:

No YouTube Logo

The logo is now removed from the player. The only time you will see the YouTube logo is when a user moves their mouse over the player. The logo then appears in the upper right corner.

Remove Everything from a YouTube Video (Well, almost everything)

Look at the video below:

Other than the deer-in-headlights look I have in this video, what else do you see, or more importantly don't see? There's no player. Also, you can't see it but this video automatically started playing and there's no related videos at the end. If I bring my mouse over the screen, I won't get the same result as the modest branding version. Instead I'll get a small YouTube logo that fades up in the bottom corner and it will fade out when the mouse leaves the screen. Here's how it looks with the mouse hovering over the screen:

http://www.MarcBullard.com

Clicking on the screen will pause/play the video. Clicking on the YouTube link will send people to the video on YouTube. This is really cool customization of the YouTube player. Not only would this would be perfect for sales letters, but if you created an unlisted link (page 23), you could embed videos such as video products or webinar replays to only specific people. There's many uses for this.

So do you want to know how to do it? I'm not going to tell you. Just kidding. It is a little complicated so what I'm going to do is provide you with the code already made and you just need to replace one thing. Nice huh?

The code looks like this:

```
<iframe width="560" height="349"
src="http://www.youtube.com/embed/39pjOe5e0m8?rel=0;autoplay=1;contro
ls=0;showinfo=0;modestbranding=1; "frameborder="0"
allowfullscreen></iframe>
```

http://www.MarcBullard.com

Now don't let this scare you, there's only one tiny part you need to change and that's the section in bold (**39pjOe5e0m8**). So what you would do is copy this entire code and paste it somewhere safe. Then go to YouTube and find the video you want to embed. Once you find the video, get that video's code. You can find the code in 2 easy places, either at the end of the URL in your browser or in the share link.

 www.youtube.com/watch?v=VzfgcKLMve0&feature=feedrec_grec_ii

Here is your ID in your browser

Link to this video:

http://youtu.be/VzfgcKLMve0

Here is your ID in the share link

Once you have your ID copied, replace the ID I have in **bold** with yours. Then copy and paste the entire code into your blog or website. There you have it, your very own playerless, logoless*, sleek looking video from YouTube.

Many businesses were hesitant to use YouTube because of some of the features they thought they couldn't change. With these features removed now, YouTube is a great decision to use on all of your sites and products. Look at it as free video hosting. Neat, YouTube even can save you money!

Equipment and video tips

Although this section could be a book in itself (Easy Web Video by Marc Bullard) I felt I needed to cover at least the basics of equipment and how to set your video up.

Equipment is a subject that gets people nervous, but it need not be. If you break it down, you really only need 4 different components to create quality looking videos.

Camera

The camera is obviously one of the most important factors into creating a very nice looking video. Believe it or not, you don't need an expensive camera. All you need is a compact, hand held camera like a Flip cam. HOWEVER, I highly recommend you **do not** get the Flip video brand. Why? Because they don't contain one extremely important component that you absolutely must have, and that is a microphone input jack. All of the Flip brand video cameras are missing this vital option. Other portable, Flip type cameras do have microphone inputs so make sure the camera you get has one.

So why is a small thing like a microphone jack so important? Well, believe it or not, audio is almost more important than your video. If you have a great shot but your audio is barely there, your video is not worth anything. However, if you have good audio but a bad picture, you can fix your shot in the editing stage. All you'd have to do is cut away to something else, such as your product, and then cut back to the video once your original shot looks good again.

Other features you will want in a camera deal with the quality of the picture. Make sure that whatever one you choose, it is shooting in HD. There are many inexpensive, available cameras that now shoot in 1080. Get one of those.

http://www.MarcBullard.com

You will also want to make sure the base of your camera has a threaded area so you can attach it to a tripod. The threaded area will screw right into your tripod, or in other cases, to a plate that will snap into your tripod. Most of these Flip type cameras have this option but don't overlook this.

You don't have to spend a ton of money in order to create a video that looks very good. Start out with the right equipment now and you'll be making videos for a long time.

Find out what camera we recommend and how to shoot with it in order to create Hollywood style videos.

Microphone

Audio is highly important to good videos. If you have bad audio, your video could be unusable. There are three different types of microphones: Handheld, Boom, and Lavalier. Lavalier is the type we are going to use. These mics are the small, newsroom type microphones that clip onto clothing. They come in either wired or wireless. Lavaliers are perfect because they can't be seen and pick up the talent's voice and not much else.

Lights

Lights can make or break the credibility of a video. Using lights correctly adds to the quality of your production and it doesn't take a lot of money. There are certain lighting techniques that you can use with 3, 2, even 1 light only and your production will still look great. Be sure to learn how to light correctly and your quality production will virtually be complete.

Editing Software

Editing software can be a daunting experience if you don't know what you're doing. I've had the privilege of using at least 10 different editing programs ranging from professional to free and I have found the best bang for your buck. Actually, there are three different programs that are almost identical in features and price. The three programs are:

• Sony Vegas Movie Studio Platinum
• Adobe Premiere Elements
• Final Cut Express

If you have any of these programs, you are in a good spot to create as many videos as you want. If you are thinking about purchasing one of these programs, they all have their own way of doing things. Once you get one of these editing programs, you will need to get training on how to quickly and easily edit your videos. And believe it or not, there are really only 3 steps you need to take in order to edit your video for the web.

YouTube Optimization and Marketing Techniques – Summarized

Now that you know how to use all of the features on YouTube, it's time to start implementing some marketing techniques. There are many different marketing techniques out there, you'll need to determine how many and what methods you want to use. But again, none of these techniques will have as much marketing power as they could if you don't optimize your videos and YouTube channel. Here's a quick list of everything you should optimize. Optimizing is highly recommended for every video.

1. File name – Put a keyword in the name of your video file before you upload to YouTube.
2. Username – If you can manage, get keywords in your channel username.
3. Title – Keywords in title. General Category – Sub Category
4. Description – URL and keywords.
5. Tags – keywords, keyword phrases, secret tag.
6. Channel – Description (About section), Tags, Website URL.
7. Playlist – Keywords in playlist name. Keywords or URL in notes.

Marketing Techniques

There are a lot of different video marketing techniques online. Feel free to search for more than what's just on this list. Again, pick and choose what techniques you want to implement. Just be sure to do something to help get your videos seen. This list outlines how each technique is supposed to work. Use the other sections of this book if you need assistance on the technical side of things.

Default Uploads – Default uploads will help make it very easy to optimize videos almost instantly. On the 'Default Uploads' page, enter information that you know you will use almost all of the time with new videos. One way to use this feature is to create some paragraphs for your video's description. These paragraphs should contain keywords related to your business. Once this description is saved in your default uploads, whenever you upload a new video, this description will already be there. Then, all you need to do is add a paragraph that is relevant to your video and that's it, your description is done. You can also save common tags that you always use in 'Default Uploads'. Feel free to set up 'Default Uploads' however you want. Also, you can still go in to each individual video and customize the title, description, and tags as much as you want.

Partnerships – Make partnerships with other YouTube users. Find users that also talk about your niche and strike a deal with them. You create a video that mentions or promotes them, their channel, etc. In return, they will create a video that showcases you. This is a great way to get new subscribers for both partners.

Up the Numbers – The more videos you make and upload, the more views and search visibility you will have. Keep making videos that contain great, usable content.

YouTube Live Events – YouTube Live is a live streaming service offered by YouTube for users to use. You can use YouTube Live Events to stream live video on the Internet. This a great platform to interact with viewers right there on the spot.

 Subscriber Messages - When you upload a new video, add a message in the subscriber message area to increase awareness. If you get a rush of subscribers to your video when you upload it, YouTube recognizes this and thinks your video must be popular. The more popular your video is, the higher it will place the video in YouTube's search results.

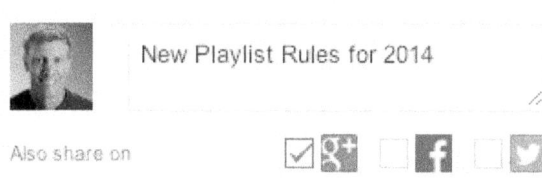

New Playlist Rules for 2014

Also share on

Subscriber message box.

PLAYLIST MARKETING

Create a playlist of some of your videos. Choose the videos based on certain topics. For instance, if you have a dog training channel and you have a few videos on the subject of puppy training, you could make a playlist for just the puppy videos. Give the playlist a title that contains keywords. Fill out the description for the playlist with keywords and keyword phrases. Add a note to each video. Contain keywords/phrases in the notes. Find competitor's videos that have a large number of views. Add one of your competitor's videos to your playlist. Doing this, people may stumble upon your videos by watching the higher ranked, competitor videos. Also, people may associate your content with the more popular, higher ranked videos. This helps build credibility. Make as many playlists as you want.

URL in comments – Any time you can get your URL visible on YouTube is a good thing. There is a way to get your URL visible in any comment that you make. It won't be clickable but hey, it's still some place that people can see your URL. Also, not many people know this technique so you are one of the lucky few that can take advantage of it.

First, you need to find a video that you want to leave a comment on. Marketing wise, it helps if this video is related to your business topic.

Next, create a playlist. If you want to combine some playlist marketing into this as well, combine related videos into this playlist.

http://www.MarcBullard.com

Add the video you want to comment on into your playlist.

View your playlist. This is very important, you must watch your playlist as if you were any other viewer.

Comment on the video (while watching your playlist). Once you post your comment, it will show up with the title of your playlist. Your title has the URL.

Marc Bullard   1 second ago
Good, simple information. Good job getting nice, clean system audio too.
Reply · 👍 👎   in playlist www.MarcBullard.com - How to Use Garageband

ANNOTATION MARKETING
You can use annotations in fun and creative ways to market your business.

Video Menu – Use annotations to create a video menu. This means you create a video, usually consisting of a still image. Once uploaded, you create annotation 'buttons' that make certain sections clickable. These clickable links go to videos, playlists, or your channel. The possibilities with video menus are endless. The nice thing about video menus is that not only does it add to your list of videos – another place for keyword optimization – but it's a neat novelty that not many users do. On top of that, it's a nice way for your viewers to access many of your videos. You can also place this menu into a playlist. That makes it easy for viewers to click the exact video they want.

http://www.MarcBullard.com

This menu has four clickable areas that link to different playlists. The clickable areas are annotation boxes.

Cliffhanger Videos – Cliffhanger videos also use annotations. Create a video but don't include the ending. Upload the ending as a separate video. On the first video, create an annotation for viewers to click that takes them to the ending. This way you can create more viewer interaction and have more than one video with similar keywords on your channel. Cliffhangers are also helpful in keeping visitors on your website by keeping them there longer. The longer a person stays on your website, the better it is in the eyes of the search engines.

http://www.MarcBullard.com

Cliffhanger videos are also great for longer videos. Longer videos can sometimes be problematic; viewers may not watch it if it's too long. Break up this long video into multiple parts that all connect to each other via annotations. This way, you can use different keywords for each part, thereby spreading the SEO power of these videos. Also, a lot of the time viewers may stumble upon one of the multiple parts. This can help get them hooked on your content. Make sure it's easy for them to get to the other parts of your video.

Subscribe and Next Video Links – Use annotations to display links that take users to other videos of yours. Also, use annotations to provide a 'Subscribe' link to your viewers.

Link to Older Videos – Use annotations to link to older videos you already have up on YouTube. This helps breathe new life into your older videos and increases views.

External Annotations – You can use an annotation to link to your website. This is a very powerful annotation and should be used in as many videos as you can.

BRANDING
Branding may not help you in the search results but it is still very powerful to get people interested in you and your products.

Fan Finder – Create a fan finder video that will get people interested in your channel. Use this video to tell people what your channel is about, why they should subscribe, how often new videos are uploaded, and any other information they may need to know. Fan Finder is free to use.

Custom Thumbnails – Custom thumbnails will really help make your videos stand apart. You can create a custom thumbnail for each video you upload. Not only will this help with branding but it can also increase views. If you have an interesting and engaging thumbnail for your video (other than a still from your video) people may be inclined to click. Most successful thumbnails use colors, an image, and text to identify what that video is about.

Example of a custom thumbnail

Channel Banner – Your channel banner is a great place to brand yourself and your business. It is also a very good place to tell people what your channel is about and how often new videos are uploaded. Use your banner to show visitors your products and introduce yourself.

This banner graphic tells visitors about the channel, upload schedule and provides a clickable link to a website.

COMMENT MARKETING
You want to try and get conversations going on YouTube. YouTube pays attention to videos that people are commenting on. This will help you in the search results.

Comment Responses to Your Videos – In your videos, make a request for others to respond with a comment or video response. These video responses can be added via YouTube or you could ask for viewers to email them to you, then you could edit them into future videos of your own. It's as simple as saying in your video "If you have any questions or want to do a video on XYZ, leave a message in the comments". You can also request viewers 'like' your video and share your video. Just ask them to do it.

Comments – Make helpful, interesting, or memorable comments to others' videos. The more helpful the comment is, the better chance you have of somebody clicking your username. You can also add comments to your own channel as well as make comments to other user's channels.

WATCH TIME – Yes, the number of views is important for marketing but not nearly as important as how long a viewer is watching your video. It is recommended that you keep your videos short and sweet as well as informative. Give viewers what they want with minimal fluff and you will have happy viewers that stay to the end of your video. The better audience retention your videos have, the higher valued they are in YouTube's eyes.

#1 MOST IMPORTANT MARKETING STRATEGY YOU CAN IMPLEMENT ON YouTube

All of the above marketing techniques are powerful and highly recommended but there is one thing you can do that will surpass everything else when it comes to your marketing efforts. Even YouTube itself suggests you do this to get the best bang for your marketing buck. So what is it?

<u>Constantly Create Content and Schedule Uploads.</u>

You really need to create fresh, new content constantly. A YouTube channel that has a video being uploaded to it once a month (every month) will do better than a YouTube channel that uploads 5 videos at once every 6 months. YouTube wants channels that are constantly pushing out new videos on some sort of schedule. Similar to a TV channel that has regular broadcasting every day of the week, you want to try to do the same thing with your YouTube channel.

Now, this doesn't mean you need to have a new video on your channel every day of the week, but you need to determine some sort of schedule that will provide new content (videos) as consistently as you can. If you can do one new video a month or every two weeks, that's great.

The average schedule that most YouTubers start out with is at least one new video uploaded every week. If you have one new video on YouTube once a week it is recommended that you upload that video on the same day every week. This way viewers (and subscribers) will be able to rely on your schedule and come watch your new content. Don't forget to put a subscriber message in the message box and remember, if you have the featured enabled for scheduled uploads, you can schedule these videos to become public ahead of time.

What NOT to do

There are definitely some things you should never do on YouTube no matter how easy or time-saving they may seem.

Features or Sites that simulate video watching – There are services out there that you can use to inflate views. A lot of the time, these sites mimic real viewers. This may seem great at first but YouTube is smart and knows a lot of the tricks. If you get caught, you might lose your account. Don't do it.

Disliking/Flagging – Don't go to your competitors and start clicking the thumbs down button. Some people take this a step further and will create multiple accounts to dislike the video as much as possible. YouTube pays attention to users that don't do anything but dislike videos.

Spam comments – If you click around YouTube long enough, you'll see comments that are clearly spam. Nobody likes these comments and it's a quick way to get your account deleted. Don't do this.

Spamming users inbox – Some people my try to spam you through your inbox. This is usually apparent when you see their video has nothing to do with your topic. Even if you are only contacted users in your field, don't use the inbox to spam them. Use it to form relationships with other users.

Get the help you need

Video may seem like it would have a steep learning curve. But if you have the proper training, including step-by-step instruction, you can quickly learn how to create and market your videos. The list below provides very basic information on creating videos.

Scripting
When it comes to online video for marketing, there are two specific categories of video you should be familiar with. The two types of videos you're going to be producing are:

1. Videos that welcome people to your website

2. Videos that market and drive traffic to your website.

They are two totally different styles, not necessarily in the way they look or any of the framing or lighting or things that I'm going to talk about.
You always want them to be as nice as they possibly can on each one of those. But you just want to keep in mind that you are trying to drive traffic so you want to say different kinds of things.

The scripting is very important in terms of getting people to a website where you want to talk about benefits and the things that you have, maybe freebies that people can pick up. Usually, there is going to be an opt-in box on your website, and this is how you're going to use your videos to capture leads and build an email list.

These videos are the tool you're using to sell yourself just like a presentation, and you're going to be leading people to a conversion. A conversion could be a thing, a sign up, or a purchase. Just going to the website itself is a conversion. But videos are meant to convert so these marketing videos are made specifically to tell as much as you can without giving away everything. All of the important information is on the website.

For instance say, 'if you want to learn the secret to great leadership for teenagers so they can build a life for themselves, I have all the information over on my website.' You want to make sure that you're leading people there and not giving away too much. People will have no reason to visit the website if you've given too much information.

So it's a matter of carefully scripting, carefully leading them to the website. Now, the video that welcomes people is for introducing yourself. If someone is at the website, you get to explain what's around the website, help them navigate around by even pointing to different parts of the website like 'sign up in the box on the right-hand corner'. You may even want to reference that with your fingers or navigate around, click the different tabs to lead them around the site. So it's a virtual, visual lead around the site instead of letting them just struggle on their own.

Creating scripts for each type of video is a great idea. Once you have a basic script, all you have to do is replace the keywords in that script over and over again, creating a lot of videos quickly.

* Bonus Script Point
Many people fear they will forget what they're going to say in their video. One expensive option to consider is a teleprompter. A teleprompter projects your lines onto a screen that you can read off of. Most news stations use teleprompters. The poor man's version of a teleprompter is to take your script, print it out with large font on paper, and then tape that paper to the bottom of your camera, just out of view of the lens. Now you can read your script while the shot looks like you're simply looking at the camera.

Shooting Tips

When it comes to shooting your video, there are a few things you should take into account in order to have a great looking video.

• No striped shirts or blouses or tight patterns
Striped shirts or blouses with tight, intricate patterns can cause the camera to do some weird things. Most importantly, patterns can cause a 'shimmering' effect to the camera. This shimmering can be distracting, taking away from the viewer getting the most out of your content.

• No dangle jewelry
Jewelry that dangles can be an audio nightmare. Not only can it create an annoying jingle every time it's wiggled, it can also bump the mic. This bump can go unnoticed while shooting but can be a pain to deal with once you get to the editing stage.

• Color Choice
The color choice of your shirt can make or break your video. Strong red colors can have a harsh effect on the camera, causing the red to bleed. Depending on the background, black shirts can also be a bad idea. Good colors to consider are nice, neutral tones such as any pastel colors, light blue, grey, tan, and even brown.

• Wait a few seconds before speaking to give room at the beginning for a fade in
This tip will save you a lot of time when it comes to editing. At the beginning of your video, you may want to fade in. That is, dissolve from a black screen into the shot. When you start recording, give the camera a few seconds of recording before you start speaking. You should also do the same thing at the end of your video.

• Smile at the end
At the end of your video, be sure to smile and look right at the camera. This is a welcoming way to end your video and it gives your editor time to fade out, or to throw some graphics up on the screen.

http://www.MarcBullard.com

•Use bullet points, not a whole script
Earlier, we gave you a bonus tip about the poor man's teleprompter. Although this is still a good idea, it's not a good idea to write out your <u>entire</u> script. We've found that videos which don't have a whole script to be the best and most natural sounding video. If you really need something to help you, put bullet points on your teleprompter instead.

• Say your website without the "WWW"
Saying the name of your website on your video is a good idea. However, it can be a major tongue twister having to say the 'www' part. Leave that part out. These days, everybody knows that websites begin with 'www'.

Sticky Sites
How long someone stays on a website is one of the determining factors of search positioning. Google likes to know that people are staying on a website. The average is six seconds for someone to visit a website and then leave but if they're on there for 30 seconds or more the search engines realize that people are staying there because this site must be good and it must have information that is critical to them. I call that stickiness.

You want your site to be sticky. Stickiness is also good for your Youtube channel. Two ways to make your channel sticky are: 1. Create engaging videos that keep your viewer watching for as long as you can keep them, and 2. Put as many videos on your channel as you can, giving your viewers more options.

Design of Video

Backgrounds

Backgrounds are important. The most important factor I'm talking about here is complementary backgrounds. The background conveys an unconscious visual stimuli in the viewers so they know that you're the expert on something. For instance, if you are a lawyer, you should be sitting at a desk with some books behind you that make you look knowledgeable, not in a funeral parlor or something that doesn't have anything to do with a lawyer.

If you do have a distracting background, such as a funeral parlor, people get distracted and start asking themselves, "Why is he at a funeral parlor? I wonder why he's at a funeral parlor?" Meanwhile they're missing a lot of important content.

Closing Credits

This book could easily double in size if I were to go into detail about the actual production process of making your videos. Hopefully, you either know what you are doing when it comes to creating videos or you have some sort of help in doing so. If you are neither inclined in video production or in contact with somebody who is, don't despair, there is help out there. One great place to get help is to contact me, the author of this book, Marc Bullard. You can email me at bullard.marc@gmail.com or feel free to check out my website MarcBullard.com to discover everything I can do for you.

Also, for more information on video production, video marketing, or online marketing in general feel free to check out these sites. I am a contributor to all of them:

MarcBullard.com
YouTube Channel – videoMTC

http://www.MarcBullard.com

Marc's Google+
YouTube Marketing Mastery (video training)

Hopefully, with the information in this book, you will be well on your way to gaining customers through the ever-growing world of YouTube. Best of luck!

About the Author

Marc Bullard has over 15 years of combined experience with video production, online businesses, and video marketing. He has a Bachelor's degree in Video Production from Stevenson University and a Master's in Education with Technology from Ashford University. Currently, he is the 'video guy' for Internet marketing guru Tom Antion. Marc also runs a marketing blog. If you would like consulting and virtual assistance services with Marc, check out his blog.

In his spare time Marc likes to be at the beach, especially surfing, or hanging out with his wife Kara, chasing after his three year old son Nateo, and caring for his crazy 1 year old baby boy Vann.

http://www.MarcBullard.com

Notes

www.ingramcontent.com/pod-product-compliance
Lightning Source LLC
Chambersburg PA
CBHW051642170526
45167CB00001B/297